MW00849016

THROUGH FLAMING SWO. of the founder of the Friends Church, and Arthur O. Roberts clearly articulates the beliefs and formative spiritual experiences of George Fox. In the final and most extensive chapter, Roberts skillfully traces the testimonies of other prominent Friends leaders and sets forth major tenets of Friends faith and practice (the redeeming Christ, holiness, the church as covenant community, peacemaking, and ministry). Roberts has indeed made an extraordinary contribution to Christian history and beliefs.

DAVID KINGREY
*director of leadership development, Evangelical
Friends Church—Mid America Yearly Meeting
Wichita, Kansas*

GEORGE FOX, a young adult when he first experienced openings that led to the rise of Quakerism, is an inspirational and influential figure. His message of discontent and disconnect with the world continues to speak to Friends, young and old, while reminding us that the other side of the flaming sword is the paradise of God. The most significant contribution of this classic work is the final chapter, "Legacy," which focuses on Fox's doctrines of holiness and the church and how they have influenced Quaker leaders past and present.

KATIE TERRELL
*young adult Friend and
editor of* Quaker Life *magazine
Richmond, Indiana*

A BEAUTIFULLY ROUNDED account of George Fox's life—historical, biographical, personal, and spiritual, all in one. Exciting and easy to read, using many familiar but often neglected passages from the *Journal*. The book broadens out into a magnificent essay rooting the particularities of Quakerism deep in the broader evangelical tradition. Fresh as when it first appeared.

JOHN PUNSHON
author and lecturer
Milton Keynes, England

I LOVE THIS BOOK. In Roberts's engaging prose, Fox's vision for the church as a prophetic community is fresh and inspiring. May we read and heed. I'm grateful to now have copies to share while guarding my well-marked 1959 hardback edition.

CHUCK ORWILER
pastor, First Denver Friends
Denver, Colorado

A READER CAN find in this book a prominent evangelical Quaker scholar's reflections on important theological issues that continue to spark controversy among members of the Society of Friends. Were Friends to discuss these issues honestly and sincerely, the happy result might well be a move toward resolution of some of these matters—something to be greatly desired by this Friend anyway.

H. LARRY INGLE
author of First Among Friends—George Fox
and the Creation of Quakerism
Chattanooga, Tennessee

SOME BOOKS are timeless, and this is one! A half-century ago Arthur O. Roberts breathed life back into the Quaker message of holiness in his brilliant interpretation of George Fox's life and thought. Since then many reinterpretations of George Fox and Quaker history have come and gone, but this work remains a classic. We can be ever grateful that Roberts shows us so clearly that the central thrust of the Quaker message is the same as that of the gospel: Holiness is transformation—available to everyone by grace through faith—not a legal transaction or a moral achievement we attain by trying harder, but a process of rebirth empowered by the Holy Spirit.

CAROLE SPENCER
*director of Friends Center; adjunct professor
of church history and spiritual formation,
George Fox Evangelical Seminary
Portland, Oregon*

EACH GENERATION has to relearn timeless truth. George Fox transformed the world with the power of truth. Our generation yearns and cries out for a prophet in the wilderness, as many previous generations of Quakers have. We indeed need another George Fox—an unwavering servant, and a lover of Jesus. Arthur O. Roberts echoes Fox's call to holiness, righteousness, and to the true church—headed by none other than Christ. And this is what we need most—Jesus Christ as our Prophet, Priest, and King. Are we up for it?

CHASE E. WILLCUTS
*student, George Fox University
Newberg, Oregon*

UNDERSTANDING GEORGE FOX and the times that shaped him is essential to comprehending the earliest Friends' prophetic, unique expression of the Christian gospel. That understanding is equally important for knowing how to continue a relevant, lived proclamation of that message in the 21st century. Arthur O. Roberts's update of *Through Flaming Sword* is immensely helpful on both scores.

The book is a beautifully distilled gift to busy seekers and teachers who often eye Fox's *Journal* on their shelf and promise themselves, "next month."

Reading *Through Flaming Sword* made me glad all over again to have been led in young adulthood to people who knew, taught, and lived this holistic message of experiential spiritual transformation.

RON FERGUSON
copastor, Winchester Friends Church
Winchester, Indiana

THIS CONCISE VOLUME is a welcomed invitation to once again receive challenge and inspiration from the life of George Fox and the early Quaker movement. Arthur O. Roberts has mined Fox's journal for the gems that reflect light on our present individual and corporate journeys. In doing so, he makes accessible for young and old the lives of a people who lived in the power of the Holy Spirit. The contributions of the Quaker perspective of holiness and community are a tool for discernment as we work out our faith with fear and trembling.

PAUL BOCK
Friends minister
Newberg, Oregon

THIS UPDATED VERSION of *Through Flaming Sword* provides a concise summary of the history of the Friends movement as well as demonstrates its ongoing relevance in today's emerging culture. I especially appreciate Roberts's emphasis on the need to recapture the original Quaker approach to holiness, which places equal weight on both the experiential and ethical dimensions of Christian discipleship. It is this ageless "holistic holiness" that lies at the heart of the Friends experience and every other authentic expression of Christianity.

DAVID WILLIAMS
*associate professor of pastoral
ministries/college chaplain, Barclay College
Haviland, Kansas*

THE BEST starting point for understanding the Friends Church is the person of George Fox, and an excellent starting point for understanding George Fox is Arthur O. Roberts's *Through Flaming Sword*. More than a mere repetition of Fox's *Journal*, Roberts tells the story of Fox's life, convictions, and contribution to the Friends movement in a highly readable and concise form using a variety of original sources and his own insightful commentary. Of special interest to thoughtful evangelicals will be Roberts's essays on a Christ-centered holiness and the priority of the church among early Friends.

JIM LESHANA
*senior pastor, Rose Drive Friends Church
Yorba Linda, California*

THERE ARE MANY heroes and geniuses of Christian spirituality, but few of them rise to the level of George Fox. Prophet, founder, theologian, and spiritual activist, Fox sets a high standard to meet. Arthur O Roberts's delightful book, *Through Flaming Sword*, combines sterling and accessible biographical writing with some of the most compelling theological exegesis I've run across in a long time. Inspiring, challenging, and compelling, this little book will prove a treasure for all readers, Quaker and non-Quaker alike.

CHRIS FAATZ
Powell's Books
Portland, Oregon

Introduction

GEORGE FOX left his mark on the world in many ways. A strange man and a religious genius, he elicited many and varied opinions. The Quaker Awakening, which sprang from his spirit and leadership, has profoundly influenced the church—its teachings, worship, and witness. It is true, also, that in the cozy alcove of contemporary Quakerism people quite unlike Fox in belief and experience have found a haven. Some restless religious sophisticates crave novelty. Most, however, seek a kind of Christianity uncluttered by form and symbol, wherein they can experience a close relationship with Jesus Christ, the present Lord and Teacher.

Regardless of what causes interest, fascination with the movement continues. Over the past three-and-a-half centuries lay and scholarly interest in Fox has continued. The focus of that interest varies—mysticism, peacemaking, meditative worship, social justice, humanitarian concerns, doctrinal clarity, or personal spirituality.

How, or whether, these interests fit within normative Quaker thought may best be discerned from the life and writings of George Fox. Knowledge about George Fox comes best by reading his writings, *Journal*, "Doctrinals," letters, and polemics. The first six chapters of this book follow the *Journal*. The final chapter, "Legacy," in large measure consists of essays about two significant doctrinal features of George Fox's experience of Jesus Christ—the nature of Christian holiness and the nature of the church. Much of this material draws upon my early studies, "The Concepts of Perfection in the History of the Quaker Movement"[1] and "George Fox's Concept of the Church."[2] It also utilizes his other writings (often neglected) as well as the works of his contemporaries.

The sentence structure of Fox's writings may seem awkward to current readers, as it did to critical contemporaries. Some of his writing became the butt of jokes by more sophisticated writers: They blamed printers for making their works look like Fox's pamphlets! It helps to know that the *Journal* was dictated by Fox from jails to young folks who were inexperienced or loath to change phrases around. And the literary style of the 17th century was more verbose than contemporary prose. But when one seeks enduring marks of literary excellence—simplicity, metaphoric power, and nobility of thought—the *Journal* ranks high in literary beauty, the beauty of a searching soul finding and serving God. Think about this when you read quotations from Fox and other early Friends in the pages that follow.

What is my desire for this book? To make available to contemporary readers a spiritual biography of a person whose passionate and insightful ministry, for more than three-and-a-half centuries, has influenced the world greatly. George Fox is respected as a courageous, God-touched man who ably articulated biblical truth about vital Christian faith and practice at a critical time in history; who led a spiritual awakening that drew thousands of people to Christ; and who set in motion a creative, worldwide covenant community, now known as Friends, or Quakers.

I gratefully acknowledge the many writers whose contributions have been influential, although indirect, and those scholars whose writings the footnotes credit. I extend my

When I came to eleven years of age, I knew pureness and righteousness; for while I was a child I was taught how to walk so as to be kept pure. The Lord taught me to be faithful in all things, and to act faithfully...inwardly to God and outwardly to man; and to keep to yea and nay in all things.[6]

So as he grew up, George followed these rules of honest speech and healthful living that later proved of incalculable value in giving him moral and physical stamina. His covenant with God prohibited him to waste anything, but to make all glorify God.

"If George says 'Verily,' there is no altering him."

It is small wonder some of his relatives wanted this world-shunning boy to become a priest. But "others persuaded to the contrary," among whom—this is only a guess —may have been his mother. Instead, while still hardly more than a boy, George was apprenticed to a shoemaker. This does not indicate the Fox family was poverty-stricken. They were probably above-average in economic status. His weaver father and cultured mother were not aristocrats, but they lived comfortably. All boys learned a trade—it was part of the educational process—so George learned to cut leather, to sew, and to peg shoes. His employer also kept sheep and cattle, grazing them and selling them. The teenage boy became so trusted that he handled much of the business and the trading. While he remained with the shoemaker-cattle-trader, business boomed, but after George left the man went broke.

As George grew toward his latter teens, he became increasingly aware of the hollowness of religious life around him. People laughed at his honesty; but they trusted him. They scoffed at his clean-mindedness; but they loved him.

3

But because they troubled him—and because, no doubt, he troubled them—George began to walk more and more alone. He had to think things through. Each week of his life as a boy and youth, he attended the Drayton church. During these years he had heard long sermons by Puritan preachers. Nathaniel Stephens, an Oxford scholar of some ability, came to Drayton at the age of thirty-four to be the minister during the impressionable years before Fox left the church. Although George received little formal schooling, he was not uneducated. He read much, no doubt, for his writings show a wide interest, and during his lifetime he accumulated quite an extensive library for one whose circumstances were so narrowed. He was, nevertheless, essentially spiritually minded. He knew the Bible so well that he could quote most of it by memory.

He received much of this Bible-centered education through expositions in church and at home. Some who see only the mature Christian experience of the man forget his solid scriptural grounding. His vision and insight followed a thorough grounding in Scripture. It was tested in the laboratory of his spirit during quiet times alone with God.

So it was that as a growing youth the sensitivity of George Fox clashed with an ugly world—a harsh, violent, and hypocritical one. The ethical example of his father and the love demonstrated by his mother had merged with his own experience of God at the age of eleven. At nineteen, the youth discovered arrayed against him a strong denial of all he held true and good. The denial came through the open and careless contempt many of his associates exhibited for clean, holy living. The denial came, too, from his own Puritan environment that had camouflaged its legal loopholes with erudite theological speculations, so that "a wayfaring man, though a fool," need not err in finding a way to continue in sin while claiming to be a Christian! When the realization and the clergy moved in. "Priest" Nathaniel Stephens, an Oxford-educated Puritan minister, came often to visit George, and George went often to talk with his pastor. The discussions were over theology, for George was seeking to reconcile the darkness of human experience with the salvation God offers. The learned pastor asked Fox once why Jesus said, "Father, if you are willing, take this cup from me; yet not my will, but yours be done" (Luke 22:42). To this troubled but perceptive young George responded:

> I told him; at that time the sins of all mankind were upon him, and their iniquities and transgressions, with which he was wounded; which he was to bear and to be an offering for, as he was man, but died not as he was God; so, in that he died for all men, tasting death for every man, he was an offering for the sins of the whole world. This I spoke, being at that time in a measure sensible of Christ's sufferings.[4]

Pastor Stephens used these conversations as a basis for some Sunday morning sermons. No one appreciates being "used," and George got irked that his pastor would exploit his existential angst as a case study, or spar with him in intellectual debate, instead of helping him realize an experiential relationship with Christ. Stephens later became a persecutor of Fox.

After losing faith in this advisor, Fox went to an elderly preacher at Mancetter, in Warwickshire. But the old gentleman, ignorant of George's need, advised tobacco and psalm-singing to cure melancholia. Also, as a wise spiritual "householder," he brought from his treasures things both new and old. But, records Fox, "Tobacco was a thing I did not love, and psalms I was not in a state to sing; I could not sing."[5]

After this old man had broadcast George's troubles "among the milk-lasses," as Fox so graphically put it, the thirsty pilgrim hunted up a priest (minister) of Tamworth, who was recommended for his counseling techniques! But George found him to be "like an empty hollow cask."

Dr. Cradock, of Coventry, when approached by the despondent youth, catechized him—asking him, for example, who Jesus' father and mother were. To this George replied that Mary was Jesus' mother and that Jesus was the Son of God. Clearly it wasn't heresy that caused the lad's sufferings, as the good doctor probably suspected. While walking together through the garden, along a narrow path between the flower beds, George awkwardly trampled a precious plant with his foot. This so upset the advisor, Fox declared, that "he raged as if his house had been on fire."

George tried one more minister. This one, named Macham, had a therapeutic turn of mind. He suggested the remedy then in vogue—physic and bloodletting, a combination horrid enough to cure or to kill! But the Lord in mercy spared Fox the ordeal of bloodletting at least, for as Fox writes:

> They could not get one drop of blood from me, either in arms or head...my body being, as it were, dried up with sorrows, grief and troubles, which were so great upon me that I could have wished I had never been born, or that I had been born blind, that I might never have seen vanity and wickedness, and deaf, that I might never have heard vain and wicked words, or the Lord's name blasphemed.[6]

Why no blood came is a question for psychosomatic medicine to explain. It's better to understand it as Fox's empathetic anguish. He *felt* the burden of wickedness. He *sensed* somewhat the sufferings of Christ. But his eyes had not yet lifted from the valley of death to the divine hills of deliverance.

George looked no longer for pastoral counseling. Like the old shepherds of Israel in Jesus' time, to this young man these seemed blind leaders of the blind. So, during that year,

1646, he trudged about the marshy fenland distributing money to needy widows and young married couples, avoiding Christmas season frivolity, and waiting for "openings" from the Lord.

"None were true believers but such (as). . . were all born of God."

This realization came to Fox through an "opening." Whether in Protestant or Catholic settings, new birth—not church membership, baptism, and rituals—is what makes people Christian. Given this insight George quit attending the little village church at Drayton. Instead, on Sunday mornings he would tuck a Bible under his arm and hike out to an orchard to read and to pray. On one such meditative morning the Lord spoke to him to this effect: "That being bred at Oxford or Cambridge was not enough to fit and qualify men to be ministers of Christ." Why, then, should he listen to Stephens? For a minister must first be anointed and taught of the Lord; and the Lord did not dwell in temples or church buildings, but in people's hearts. This realization provided a beacon light, as if drawn to truth by Bethlehem's star. The direction of Fox's search then shifted. He had sought in the words of others a satisfying rational proposition; now he looked for help directly from God.

People, of course, became aware that *some* sort of divine presence surrounded Fox. They came to look upon him as a discerner of truth amid a social clutter of pretense. And so the wandering youth began to converse with individuals and groups of folk hungry for something better than the state church. Even then, he was actually still a wandering seeker, for although he had many openings, and although Scriptures were unfolded to him, he remained troubled. "When it was day I wished for night," he remembered, "and when it was

1 1

night I wished for day." His practice was to remain in a town a short time, and then move on to another, sojourning among the Dissenters for a time in hopes of finding the fellowship in the spirit that he was seeking. But he was disappointed in his hopes.

"There is one, even Christ Jesus, that can speak to thy condition."

His dealings with the dissenting people convinced him there was much good among them, that they were "tender people," but that he must seek help elsewhere. This help did come, and light did flood down to dispel the darkness of his despair. The light he discovered is Christ—the risen and present Lord. Here are his words:

> And when all my hopes in them and in all men were gone, so that I had nothing outwardly to help me, nor could I tell what to do; then; oh! then I heard a voice which said, "There is one, even Christ Jesus, that can speak to thy condition:" and when I heard it, my heart did leap for joy. Then the Lord did let me see why there was none upon the earth that could speak to my condition, namely, that I might give Him all the glory; for all are concluded under sin, and shut up in unbelief, as I had been, that Jesus Christ might have the preeminence, who enlightens, and gives grace, faith, and power. Thus when God doth work, who shall let hinder it? This I knew experimentally. My desires after the Lord grew stronger, and zeal in the pure knowledge of God, and of Christ alone, and without the help of any man, book, or writing. For though I read the Scriptures that spake of Christ and of God, yet I knew Him not, but by revelation, as He who hath the key did open, and as the Father of Life drew me to His Son by His Spirit. Then the Lord gently led me along, and let me see His love, which was endless and eternal.[7]

In experiencing so dramatically the *assurance* of the Savior, George Fox no longer feared the ungodly people of the fenlands, no longer felt threatened by hypocrisy or scoffing unbelief. No longer a burdened seeker, he became a joyous "finder"—a finder of Christ, the highest treasure of the heart! Gone was the darkness of his own soul! In the light of Christ he found faith, and trust, and hope, and love. That spiritual experience he had been seeking came when he turned from human counsel and opened his heart to assuring grace from the nail-scarred hands of the living Christ. This was the key that set him free.

In the inevitable temptations that assailed him during the following months of 1647, George Fox received the reassurance that the tempter could be overcome "in and by Christ." He came to experience God as a refining fire in which his thoughts were discerned and cleansed from evil. He learned what it meant for "self" to be cut down by the sword of the Spirit. By the year 1648, his spiritual trials seemed to be over so that he could exult in this paean packed with powerful biblical imagery:

> Now was I come up in Spirit, through the flaming sword, into the paradise of God. All things were new; and all the creation gave another smell unto me than before, beyond what words can utter. I knew nothing but pureness, innocency, and righteousness, being renewed up into the image of God by Christ Jesus; so that I was come up to the state of Adam, which he was in before he fell....But I was immediately taken up in Spirit, to see into another or more steadfast state than Adam's in innocency, even into a state in Christ Jesus, that should never fall. The Lord shewed me, that such as were faithful to him, in the power and light of Christ, should come up into that state in which Adam was before he fell.[8]

The divine-human double search was over. At age twenty-three George Fox was ready to face England and the world with a message of victory over sin through Jesus Christ. The rich experience of knowing Christ experimentally, which had flashed across his path, was sustained by the rich store of knowledge he had acquired through long and careful reading of the Bible and through his wanderings among Puritans and Separatists. The sect of the Familists, headed by Henry Nicholas, Dutch mystic, had called for the attainment of an actual holiness of life, a real righteousness. The assurance that Fox had understood rationally he now understood intuitively—with the heart. Neither instinctive nor intellectual activity sufficed to bridge the chasm between the self and God. Truth was brought within the range of human response, "but it remained essentially mysterious, an operation, gift, or grace of God dwelling in man somehow apart from his natural capacities."[9]

Fox was no ignorant prophet. Elbert Russell states that "he brought to his work at the outset of his preaching a better knowledge of theology, church history, and the Bible than many a theological student today."[10]

This once-troubled, wandering young seeker had become a possessor and preacher of a joyous gospel. If George Fox be counted a mystic, it is in this sense: An introspective space and time provided the setting for him to be drawn to Jesus Christ, who reached out to him in redemptive love and sent him forth in the power of the Holy Spirit.[11] *His* solitary seeking had been often filled with despair, not tranquil contemplation. The ingrained gregariousness of George Fox's personality required no retreat from the world, but rather an outlet within it, for active witness through word and deed. Yes, the double search was done, and the Quaker Awakening of the church had begun.

VISION
AND
FULFILLMENT

*"That which people trample upon
must be thy food."*

IN THE FIRST YEAR of his ministry, 1647, George Fox labored under the burden of the sins of mankind. He sensed that underneath vile actions were vile natures. And he cried out to the Lord, who showed him that to minister unto the people he must have "a sense of all conditions." "I saw also," reported Fox in powerful imagery, "that there was an ocean of darkness and death; but an infinite ocean of light and love, which flowed over the ocean of darkness."

Because people denied the reality of Christian experience, an ocean of darkness hovered like fog over swampy marshes. "They fed upon words, and fed one another with words; but trampled under foot the blood of the son of God, which blood was my life," cried Fox.[1]

15

What is implied by such metaphoric criticism? To answer this let's review the religious situation of England in this era. The Elizabethan policy of compromise and conformity in religious affairs since 1558 had brought a temporary peace among quarrelling factions. The "Marian exiles" (those whom Catholic Queen Mary, the embittered daughter of Henry VIII and Catherine of Aragon, had harried from the land in 1553-1558) brought Calvinism back from Geneva. This meant they had different ideas about theology, church policy, and government. The church at home had known persecution under "Bloody Mary." Fox's ancestors were numbered among the three hundred Protestants who were burned at the stake, along with those famous churchmen: Latimer, Ridley, and Cranmer. England had become, for several generations by this time, a people of one book, the Bible. Puritanism, John Calvin's gift to England, fostered a groundswell of religious awakening that achieved significant influence through the wide diffusion of the Scripture to the people. Witness the long-enduring use of the King James Version of the English Bible of 1611 (even though the autocratic Stuart king had offered it as a political concession). The Puritans determined to "purify" what they considered to be the "half-Catholic" Church of England, to purge it from "idolatrous" elements. They inclined toward Presbyterian Church polity and the limited monarchy of the state. Puritanism brought to the English Reformation tender consciences and strong religious convictions. The Reformation, which hitherto had been dominated by personal, political, and traditional agendas, became infused with the spiritual force of evangelical Christianity. "Righteous Christer," Fox's father, came from such sturdy stock.

About the same time a new group of Separatists began their trek to the new world of America. During Fox's childhood the Catholic "specter" arose again, for King Charles had a Catholic wife. While Fox was growing up the nation became locked in a three-way struggle: Catholic vs. Protestant; Puritans vs. Establishment; and Nonconformist sects vs. both church and state.

By the time Fox was sixteen, civil war loomed; sides were well chosen and defined. The Cavalier party represented feudal and Tudor traditions of privileged power, divine right of kings and of Anglican bishops. It espoused an impersonal, mildly Arminian, type of Christianity (i.e., an emphasis upon free will rather than predestination). Elaborately artificial courtesies and clothing styles accentuated the superficiality of the times. The Cavaliers, privileged and debonair, patronized the arts and theatre. The opposing "Roundheads" exalted the power of parliament and the growing merchant class. They hated vice and feared God. In theory at least, they wanted a theocracy. The Long Parliament had come into power in 1640, and then the Commonwealth a few years later, which extended until 1660. Archbishop Laud was put to death in 1645, the same year that Fox had left his companions, his home, his church, in order to find peace of heart. And while Cromwell was trying to assemble the kingdom by force, Fox was finding a kingdom of truth and love beyond the flaming sword of Eden.

The religious confusions that prevailed in England ever since Henry VIII had become the head of the Church reached a boiling point during the Commonwealth interlude. Because "there was no major prophet who by inspiration, conviction, and illuminated vision could lift his nation to a new tableland of truth and experience,"[2] the period opened with a large number of sects that were tired of political contention and bickering over religious matters. John Milton, writing in 1644, said that "the shop of war hath not there more anvils and hammers...than there be pens and heads...musing, searching, revolving new notions and ideas."[3]

In this revolutionist-idealist milieu even Cromwell's army became a veritable debating society. Anabaptists, Familists, Behmenists (followers of Jacob Boehme, Saxon shoemaker and mystic, who died the year George Fox was born), Seekers, and Ranters—such were the religious groups agitating throughout the land. The Continental influences were strong in many of them. Some had experienced the chaos of the Thirty Years' War (between Lutheran and Roman Catholic forces on the continent) which came to an exhausted conclusion in 1648 with the Peace of Westphalia.

An "ocean of darkness" was not just a personal experience in the dreary Drayton countryside in the year 1647 when Fox began to evangelize: Its waves had swept over the Western world. As if by divine wrath, London suffered a terrible plague that killed thousands of people. Amid uncertainty, darkness, suffering, war, death, and fear, English people looked for hope and meaning. They looked beyond philosophers Locke, Hobbes, and Herbert; beyond literary figures Milton, Dryden, and Bunyon; beyond politicians Pym, Hampden, and Elliot; beyond military leaders Fairfax, Cromwell, and Monk; beyond scientists Newton and Harvey; beyond religionists Baxter, Taylor, Ussher, and Chillingworth. In this time of darkness they sought *spiritual* assurance of the sort Fox discovered—an "ocean of Light" giving victory over sin and restoring personal and social hope.

> *"I saw the harvest white . . .*
> *and none to gather it;*
> *for this I mourned with tears."*

Fox began his public ministry at Duckenfield and Manchester, in Derbyshire. It's in this community that he first records *convincements*—a term he used for those who were reached for the Lord through his preaching. Elizabeth Hooton was one of his converts early in that first year of ministry. She became the first to follow him in the ministry. From Derbyshire Fox went to the Baptists at Broughton, in Leicestershire, where, he writes, "the Lord's power began to spring; I had great openings in the scriptures, and several were convinced in those parts, and turned from darkness to light, and from the power of Satan unto God."[4]

In 1648 he entered Nottinghamshire and began to preach among the Ranters, Baptists, Independents, and other restless sectarians. At this time George Fox supported himself as a shoemaker. He preached at every opportunity he could find. Sometimes he preached in churches (he called them "steeplehouses") in the period after the minister's hour was up and others could legally speak. At other times he preached in houses where sectarian groups met, or on street corners and at fairs—wherever he could get an audience. At Mansfield, in Nottinghamshire, George Fox prayed with such fervor that one of those present at a great meeting reported, "It was now as in the days of the apostles, when the house was shaken where they were."[5]

Fox stayed around Mansfield for several months, and the first community of the "Children of Light," as some of the Friends were first called, began in this town. It was here, too, that Fox was "moved of the Lord" to speak to some justices— who were meeting there—regarding unjust wages for servants. He put off until morning his errand, for there were some fiddlers and entertainers at the meeting that evening and he thought it better to wait. But when morning came, he discovered that the party had already gone. He was struck blind by the emotional reaction from having neglected a leading of the Lord. Learning that the justices were at a town eight miles distant, Fox, sight now returning, ran as fast as he could in order to deliver his message to them. "They all received my exhortation kindly," he notes, "for I was moved of the Lord."[6]

19

At Mansfield the young prophet was moved to go talk to "one of the wickedest men in the country," whose identifying sins were that he was a common drunkard, a noted whoremaster, *and* a rhyme-maker! The admonition struck so sharply that the man had no strength to resist. He became and remained an honest, sober man, to the astonishment of the people who had known him before.[7] Presumably, he wrote no more rhymes!

In the course of these first three years' ministry, young Fox saw clearly that he was called to "turn people from darkness to the light, that they might receive Christ Jesus." But he also saw that none of the sects in Christendom could bear to be told that through Christ people could be made pure and without sin as Adam had been in the perfection of his innocency. Therefore, people must be drawn away from forms, and images, and crosses, and sprinklings of infants, and bowings and scrapings before nobility. All these things, he concluded, hid the reality of simple faith and trust in Jesus Christ. "I was to bring them off from all the world's fellowships…that their fellowship might be in the Holy Ghost."[8]

Like the Old Testament prophet Hosea, Fox trudged among the people and cried out against sin. He walked into courts and admonished periwigged judges to be fair. He went to markets and urged fair dealings instead of peddling deceitful merchandise, cheating, and what he called "cozening." He laid the foundation for the Quaker insistence upon a fixed price, which was later to shape England's future and to make Quaker merchants and bankers the most trusted of the land. He warned schoolteachers of their duty to teach Christian virtues. He admonished parents to instruct their children in the New Covenant as the Jews had instructed their children in the Old Covenant.

What aroused Fox to the depths of consecrated fury was the sight of the steeplehouses. One Sunday morning he heard a bell tolling from a steeple. He could stand it no longer. Slipping away from his traveling companions, he entered the service of the church to cry out against "idolatry" of forms and ceremonies. He interrupted the sermon to proclaim that as the Jews had accepted Scripture but rejected Christ, so this congregation blindly accepted Scripture without receiving Christ of which it spoke. The immediate result is recorded in this masterful bit of British understatement: "As I spoke thus amongst them, the officers came, took me away, and put me into a pitiful stinking place...where the stench of the place was in my throat and head many days after."[9]

During the furor of the trial several people were impressed by the stalwart character of Fox and were convinced by his words. By the time he ended this first imprisonment, in the Nottingham jail, there were several believers as a result of his ministry of earnest suffering, ill-advised though it may have been.

Following release from a short jail sentence (possibly as much as two or three months), Fox brought healing for a woman whom physicians were trying to bleed in order to cure her distraught mind. One who had so recently suffered could speak in quietness and calmness so that "the Lord's power settled her mind, and she mended."[10] He tells of other such instances in which his words of comfort and his simple trust in the power of Christ effected healing in tortured minds and bodies. Miracles, though recorded, were never magnified out of proportion. The total message of salvation remained uppermost.[11]

Like the early apostles, Fox was undaunted by imprisonment. Once he tried to speak in another steeplehouse. This time the people beat him with their hands, Bibles, and sticks, and finally stoned him out of town for preaching "the word of Life to them." But that day some were convinced, and for that George Fox rejoiced to be counted worthy to suffer for the sake of Christ.

At Market-Bossoth, Fox met up with former pastor, Nathaniel Stephens, who encouraged people to stone the mad preacher—Fox—out of town!

But Fox continued to display courage. At Twy-Cross back in Leicestershire, in 1649, the year that the Commonwealth executed King Charles I, a man came at Fox with a naked rapier in his hand. The *Journal* reports the outcome this way:

> I looked steadfastly on him, and said, "Alack for thee poor creature! What wilt thou do with thy carnal weapon? It is no more to me than a straw." The standers-by were much troubled, and he went away in a rage.[12]

Others were to find out that they too, could not bear the piercing gaze of this dark-eyed, tall, courageous young man.

Late in 1650, while Fox was resting in Derby among convinced Friends, he heard the sound of a bell. It was like a fire alarm for him! Inquiring what sort of a meeting would be held on this weekday, he discovered that there was to be a lecture by a colonel of the army, who was also a preacher. Fox took a couple of associates with him and went to the crowded assembly. Fox took over the meeting and spoke "what the Lord commanded." Then an officer came and led him and his associates away for nine hours of questioning. Here his doctrine of holiness met the Calvinists' doctrine head-on. After the discussion continued on for some time, Fox told them they were not to dispute about Christ, but to obey him, at which, according to Fox, "The power of God thundered among them and they did fly like chaff before it." And continuing, he gives as bold a testimony to holiness experience as Christian devotional literature affords.

> At last they asked, whether I was sanctified? I answered, Yes, for I was in the paradise of God. Then they asked me, if I had no sin? I answered, Christ my Savior has taken

away my sin; and in Him there is no sin....When they had wearied themselves in examining me, they committed me and one other man to the house of correction in Derby for six months, as blasphemers.[13]

This law against blasphemy, under which Fox was incorrectly incarcerated, was aimed at the Ranters who thought Christian experience gave them the right not only to claim to be Christ but also to do as they pleased without having their actions termed *sin*. While in jail he wrote to the priests to tell them that the gospel was no commodity to be had for a price. He wrote to judges to inquire what sort of justice it was to silence truth and well-doing. He called upon them to repent and to walk in righteousness. Those who flocked to the jail to hear him were exhorted to quit "pleading for sin" to the grave. When Justice Bennett derided Fox and his companions as "Quakers," Fox told the judge that he should tremble at the word of the Lord. The young reformer's bold testimony so took hold of the jailer that he came in penitence to Fox and accepted the faith his prisoner had proclaimed. Fox wrote letters of encouragement to people like this who became converted through his ministry.

He was such a bothersome fellow, however, that the judge and others gave him a mile liberty each day, hoping that he would escape! But Fox only used the liberty to go about the markets urging men to repent, afterward returning to jail. Fox's relatives came with bail for his release, but he would accept none of it. Fox declared he was innocent and would thus make no such admission of guilt. So he remained in jail the full six months of his term. At its close some of the soldiers clamored to have Fox become their leader. Soldiers had been converted under his ministry behind bars and drawn by the force of his personality. Accordingly, the commissioners offered George Fox a command in the army of the

Commonwealth. To this offer he replied in words that have become classic lines for Christian peacemaking:

> I told them I knew from whence all wars arose; even from the lusts, according to James' doctrine; and that I lived in the virtue of that life and power that took away the occasion of all wars.[14]

This rebuff infuriated those who thought they were doing Fox a favor. How could they cope with a man who fought only with spiritual weapons? So they clapped him into jail again, without any bed and in the company of thirty felons, where he remained for an additional six months.

Upon release he resumed public meetings. Once while journeying with friends he saw three spires pointing to the sky above Lichfield. The sight, he said, "struck at his life." Leaving his friends, he hurried that way, leaping across hedges and ditches, until he came to a hill above the city. There he took off his shoes, which he entrusted to some astonished shepherds. Even though it was winter, "The word of the Lord was like a fire" in him. He walked barefoot up and down the streets, crying, "Woe, to the bloody city of Lichfield!" To Fox it seemed he was walking through the blood of those injured by civil wars—wars in which first a minister of the king and then a minister of parliament inflicted havoc on the place. This vision represented to him all the bloodshed of Christian martyrs, sacrificed on the altars of man's carnality.[15]

To sophisticated modern folks this Ezekiel-like dramatic act is rather embarrassing. (One recalls, however, that Jesus gathering the children embarrassed his disciples). Fox is censured for this "escapade" by some writers, or excused on the grounds of emotional disturbance brought about by his recent imprisonment. Rachel Knight, following Josiah Royce, attributes this action to his unexpended energy which, having smoldered in prison, exploded in this outburst.[16] Rufus

Jones considers the Lichfield episode a recurrent symptom of the pathological depression suffered in his searching years. However named, that condition was healed and mended when young George found faith in Christ as inward and sufficient guide.[17]

It would appear to this writer that while the trip through Lichfield apparently didn't result in any conversions, it was of deep significance to Fox. It *was* abnormal, but not destructively so. Fox *was* different from other folks. The fact remains, according to his own account, that Fox considered this event a leading of the Lord and received from it a great sense of victory and peace. The episode does give deep insight into Fox's sense of concern for the suffering of humanity—a humanity led by blind guides, whose symbols, unfortunately, were for him the spires of a church building.

While in the Derby jail Fox had made contacts with certain Separatist groups in the neighborhood of Doncaster in Yorkshire, which was but a few miles from Scrooby, the original seat of the Congregational Separatists who became the Pilgrim Fathers. These people were known as Seekers. In December 1651, Fox, the scarred young warrior of peace came into these communities to heal the wounds of a "bloody Lichfield." Many were convinced. Some who became his finest helpers were enlisted in his cause. Among them were William Dewsbury, who later called his dungeons "palaces" and the bolts of his prison "precious jewels"; and James Nayler, former army officer and brilliant preacher, who one day in an excess of fanaticism brought reproach upon Quakers.

Among the Seekers he met Justice Durant Hotham, one of the foremost English disciples of Jacob Boehme. They became friends, and many of the Seekers joined forces with Fox, here in these northern English counties. But when Fox tried to preach in a cathedral the people threw him down the steps. Fox must have startled people halfway into the kingdom! Thrown down from the church steps or suffering similar abuse, he would calmly go his way, often spending snowy nights sleeping in the shelter of a haystack. Once he preached from a haystack, with the people gathered around. But before speaking he said nothing for several hours, "to famish them from words," so that when he spoke they listened and obeyed the message.[18]

In Patrington area on this 1651 trip, no one would sell Fox any food, so he went without eating for several days. Once during worship at Tickhill, a man hit this prophet of peace in the face with a brass-bound Bible. The blow brought blood gushing out, so the people—not wanting to spoil their beautiful building—dragged him out of the church, stoned him, threw him over a hedge, and took away his hat. He seemed to have felt the loss of the hat—symbol of his deference to no man—more than the beating.[19]

"The Lord let me see . . . a great people to be gathered."

In the year 1652 the visions began to be fulfilled in larger measure than ever before. The previous four years of ministry had been painful ones; the rewards were outstanding in quality, but not in quantity. Many had scoffed. He had been ridiculed. But the tide turned, not away from persecution, but to greater results. For in that year Fox met the Seekers of Westmoreland and vicinity. Here was a prepared people and a prepared preacher. The people had exalted silence and the avoidance of forms and ceremonies in order that God would once more pour out his Spirit upon them, would send them a prophet to lead them.

Fox had been a seeker. Now, having found Christ and been found by Christ, he could minister to others who had also experienced despair and were awaiting a prophetic word from God. Rufus Jones says that the meeting was like the contact of two electrodes.[20] Fox and Richard Farnsworth saw the vision of the people to be gathered. Here is the account as given in the *Journal:*

> As we travelled, we came near a very great high hill, called Pendle-hill, and I was moved of the Lord to go up to the top of it; which I did with much ado, it was so very steep and high. When I was come to the top, I saw the sea bordering upon Lancashire. From the top of this hill the Lord let me see in what places he had a great people to be gathered. As I went down, I found a spring of water in the side of the hill, with which I refreshed myself; having eaten or drunk but little several days before.[21]

At Firbank Chapel in Westmoreland, Frances Howgill and John Audland had conducted a preaching service. Later, in the afternoon George Fox sat on a rock near the chapel where, for more than three hours, more than a thousand people gathered to hear him preach about "God's everlasting truth." All of the teachers of the congregation and many of the people were convinced and accepted the newly found faith. From here he went to other meetings to show the people the "saving knowledge of Christ." During the daytime he preached and at night he instructed leaders. Fox talked with anyone who would give attention to his ministry. With some, Fox declares that he "took a Bible and opened the scriptures, and dealt tenderly with them, as one would do with a child."[22]

At Ulverston in Furnass, Fox engaged in a public controversy with a minister named Lampitt. His cogent presentation of biblical truths won over to vital Christian faith Margaret Fell, wife of Thomas Fell, of Swarthmore Hall. Judge Fell was a member of parliament and a justice of the peace. Margaret Fell was a woman of unusual culture and spiritual insight, wealthy in her own right. She had been a Seeker for twenty years. At her invitation Fox visited Swarthmoor Hall and won over the entire household, except for Judge Fell, who was away at the time. Upon his return Fell refused to heed his hot-headed advisors, but instead accepted the situation and cordially offered Swarthmoor as a meeting house for Friends. It remained a Friends headquarters for forty years. Although he himself never became a Quaker, Judge Fell sympathized with much Fox taught.

From the new headquarters at Swarthmoor, zealous new adherents organized and collected funds to support itinerant preaching. Fox brought together able young men and women for this ministry. By the spring of 1654 "Valiant Sixty" evangelists had covered the north country in the interest of "primitive Christianity revived." They fanned out into Ireland, then down to London. Everywhere they went they made converts—and they encountered persecution. Many are the heroes of this larger story, which cannot here be recounted. George Fox remained the unofficial but real leader and guide of this evangelistic movement, with Swarthmoor serving as an administrative center.[23]

Fox must have been a marvelous leader. He seemed to captivate or to infuriate people. The love that young men and women (some still in their teens) had for their leader, and for their Christ, is shown in this account as given in the *Journal*:

> Next morning I went in a boat to James Lancaster's. As soon as I came to land, there rushed out about forty men, with staves, clubs, and fishing-poles; who fell upon me, beating, punching me, and endeavouring to thrust me backward into the sea. When they had thrust me almost into the sea, and I saw they would have knocked me down in it, I went up into the middle of them, but they laid at me again, knocked me down, and stunned me. When I came to myself, I looked up and saw James Lancaster's wife throwing stones at my face, and her husband lying over me, to keep the blows and stones from me. For the people

had persuaded James' wife that I had bewitched her husband.[24]

Lancaster's wife, like many other persecutors, soon came to be convinced of the truth. In the midst of such successes, Fox was imprisoned for the third time, on generally vague charges of blasphemy, heresy, and seduction. He was placed in the lower jail, among thieves and murderers. It seems almost impossible that he could survive these jail sentences, of which there were to be eight in all, culminating in more than six years of his life. Here is the description Fox gives of the Carlisle "gaol":

> A filthy, nasty place it was, where men and women were put together in a very uncivil manner, and never a house of office [toilet] to it; and the prisoners so lousy, that one woman was almost eaten to death with lice. Yet...the prisoners were all made very loving and subject to me, and some of them were convinced of the truth....Once he [the jailer]...beat me with his cudgel....While he struck me, I was moved to sing in the Lord's power, which made his rage the more.[25]

Once a young lad, James Parnell, sixteen years of age, came to see Fox. Perhaps he heard the prisoner sing "in the Lord's power." This youth, convinced, went out to become a superb preacher for three short years, dying as a result of his own eventual imprisonment, first martyr to George Fox's high visions.

SUFFERING AND SUCCESS

"I was moved of the Lord to write a paper 'To the protector... Oliver Cromwell.'"

THE YEAR 1655 marks the beginning of a new epoch in the ministry of George Fox. After his release from Carlisle prison he had reaped rich rewards from his preaching. The Valiant Sixty had spread the gospel into Ireland and to the south of England. Francis Howgill and Edward Burrough went to London; John Camm and John Audland to Bristol; Richard Hubberthorn and George Whitehead to Norwich; and Thomas Holmes into Wales.[1] These were vigorous youth, passionately devoted to Christ. Fox himself attracted great crowds as he preached in Cumberland, Bishoprick, Northumberland, Westmoreland, Lancashire, and Yorkshire. He describes it in this way: "The plants of God grew and flourished, so by heavenly rain and God's glory shined upon them."[2]

If Fox reached his thousands, his followers collectively were speaking to tens of thousands. By 1655, *only eight years after the beginning of his ministry*, there were some fifty thousand Quaker converts to Christ, organized into little groups, ready to bear the stigma of their faith. The "Publishers of Light" were drawing crowds of three and four thousand people per gathering when the year 1655 rolled around. Two major leaders who were at that time challenging England—Oliver Cromwell and George Fox—challenged each other politically and spiritually. During that year Fox was in Leicestershire, his home country, where he may have been without honor as far as former counselor Stephens was concerned. But not in the minds of other people! Fox was too formidable now to be harried about. As St. Paul faced his political rulers, so Fox faced his. In a paper Fox wrote as a sort of pledge to Oliver Cromwell, the Commonwealth leader ("protector"), Fox denied the wearing or drawing of a carnal sword against the protector or any other man. He was no militant revolutionary bent on overthrowing the government. He was sent instead, said Fox, to turn people from darkness to light, away from violence to the peaceable gospel. Here's an excerpt from that letter:

> From under the occasion of that sword I do seek to bring people. My weapons are not carnal but spiritual, and "my kingdom is not of this world," therefore with a carnal weapon I do not fight, but am from those things dead….And this I am ready to seal with my blood."[3]

"It would be difficult," writes a biographer, "to find in any one generation in any one country two more unique and original characters than George Fox and Oliver Cromwell."[4] Both were conscious of being divinely chosen to do a great work for the Almighty; both stood in awe before God. In a loose sense of the word, both were mystics. Cromwell, a stern Puritan, had a few Seeker strains in his veins. A man of fifty-five, he had held his office for about six months. George Fox, also of Puritan background, had been softened by a law of love, rather than hardened by the law of force. He was now in his thirtieth year, tall, sharp-eyed, and weather-beaten as he stood before Cromwell. Dressed in a leather suit and broad-brimmed hat he arrived in the early morning before Cromwell was even dressed. When the two leaders met, Fox said: "Peace be in this house," a greeting which was certainly more of a prayer than a prophecy! Fox quashed malicious rumors of armed conspiracy which had reached the ears of the protector. And then Fox "spoke to him of truth," by which is meant the gospel according to Quakers. When Cromwell upbraided Fox for quarreling with ministers, the spunky Fox retorted that it was the "priests" who did the quarrelling! Cromwell seemed to agree with Fox that some "hireling" ministers cared not a whit for the spiritual nurture of the flocks, for several times the protector exclaimed, "That is true! That is very good!"

Here's how the interview came to a close:

> I told him, that all Christendom (so called) had the scriptures, but they wanted [lacked] the power and Spirit that those had who gave forth the scriptures; and that was the reason they were not in the fellowship with the Son, nor with the Father, nor with the scriptures, nor one with another. Many more words I had with him; but people coming in, I drew a little back. As I was turning, he catched me by the hand, and with tears in his eyes, said, "Come again to my house; for if thou and I were but an hour of a day together, we should be nearer one to another.[5]

As Fox went out, the captain steered him into a dining room where he was ordered by the protector to be allowed to eat with the staff. But Fox would not "eat his bread or drink his drink." When Cromwell heard this he said: "Now I see there is a people risen, that I cannot win either with gifts, honours, offices, or places; but all other sects and people I can."[6]

Fox was now at liberty. But the rapport the two men had for each other soon began to fade. As months went by Cromwell became more authoritarian and less concerned about safeguarding liberty of conscience and freedom of religious expression.

The two met on several other occasions, subsequently. But the protector feared that lenient toleration of the Quaker "heresy," as the sterner Puritan element viewed the message of Fox, would weaken his fragile grip on the government, the "Protectorate." So for pragmatic political reasons he made life hard again for these "Children of the Light," refusing to abolish compulsory tithes, permitting the oaths of allegiance, and requiring compulsory respect to churches and magistrates ("hat honor"). No wonder Fox felt keenly disappointed in Cromwell. For within a year—1656, according to the Quakers' own records—as a result of these policies directed against Quakers "there were seldom fewer than one thousand in prison in this nation for truth's testimony."[7]

Fox himself spent eight months of that year in the Launceston jail, after which he pled his cause before Cromwell, only to have the protector declare that Fox was just following a natural light; Fox could not convince him that the light was Christ and of God.[8]

*"I was never in prison
that it was not the means of bringing
multitudes out of their prisons."*

George Fox scribbled these poignant words upon the wall of that ancient cell of death, "Doomsdale" dungeon. Among all his cogent epigrams this ranks as one of the finest. The words remain, memorialized, upon the ruined walls at Launceston (Fox spelled it *Lanceston*.)[9] Because jail sentences were so frequent, much of Fox's time was spent in tangles with the law. It is especially true for the years 1655-1666. Success for the Friends came through sufferings.

By looking at the imprisonments one can see how completely Fox broke with the churches of his time—Roman, Established, and Puritan. Accordingly, he incurred the wrath of clergy, governors, and some of the common people. Inevitably, in his bold challenges to authority, he encountered harsh opposition. His first jail sentence, as noted earlier, occurred because he did illegally interrupt a service before the permitted open time. The second imprisonment, at Derby, was based on charges of blasphemy, because he declared he was sanctified, that Christ had taken away sin. The third, at Carlisle, again resulted from a charge of blasphemy. Conviction on the second count meant the penalty of banishment, with death by hanging for failure to leave the country. British law came to his defense on this occasion, however, with Justice Anthony Pearson declaring there was no evidence to support the charges. Fox's release without formal trial was hastened (although seven weeks seems long enough!) by a letter from the famous "Barebones Parliament."[10]

The fourth imprisonment—eight months in Launceston Castle—was the most terrible of all his dungeon experiences, although shorter in time than other confinements. Fox was arrested late in 1655 because he had posted some papers the military regime deemed suspicious. The Commonwealth government was unstable, and fearful of treason by its citizens. Fox and two others waited nine weeks in jail until their trial before Chief Justice Glynn. This top justice of England was offended when the Quakers refused to take off their hats. He commanded. They refused. Fox asked the worthy judge to show him any place in Scripture, in pagan practice, or on the statutes of England where doffing the hat before authorities was commanded. Well, the judge tried to trick Fox by saying the Old Testament doesn't mention hats. In rebuttal the crafty Fox quoted from the third chapter of Daniel, noting that the three children were cast into the fiery furnace by Nebuchadnezzar's command, *with their coats, hose, and hats on.* This sharp rejoinder may have evoked laughter by the court crowd, but it infuriated the judge! So, in the role of a modern Nebuchadnezzar, judge Glynn slapped the Quakers into the jail for contempt until they should pay the heavy fine. They refused to pay the jailer his "fees" for the same reason that they refused to pay the fine—they were innocent—and accordingly they were locked into a dungeon called Doomsdale, used for witches and murderers, and from which few ever came out alive. They were there thirteen days before they were permitted to finish out their sentence in the castle, but the cruelties were bad enough—too horrible, in fact, to restate.[11]

Once a young girl brought food to them in that stinking hole. And young men came from London to take Fox's dictation, for the world was to hear about this (in unpolished prose, maybe, but with razor-sharp truth).

Ponder this poignant testimony to George Fox's charismatic power: A certain follower, Humphrey Norton, once went to Oliver Cromwell and offered *his* body for that of Fox, praying that he might go to prison as a substitute for Fox and if necessary die in his stead! Deeply touched, Oliver Cromwell turned to his council members and asked: "Which of you would do so much for me if I were in the same condition?"[12] Silence was his only answer.

After Fox was released from Doomsdale, he had the liberty of the Castlegreen (but locked back in his cell at night) and on Sunday ("First-day") mornings people came to hear him preach. The protector's chaplain, Hugh Peters, noted

"They could not do George Fox a greater service for the spreading of his principles in Cornwall than to imprison him there."[13]

The fifth imprisonment was in Lancaster Castle. It lasted four months. Whereas four years earlier Fox had been suspected of illegal acts against the Commonwealth, in 1660 he was arrested at Swarthmoor on charges of insurrection. This time, because the monarchy had been restored, it was against King Charles II. Fox defended himself ably and was sent to London, on his honor. There he was released by order from the central government.

The sixth imprisonment was of one month's duration at Leicester in 1662, for refusing to take the Oath of Supremacy and Allegiance. King Charles had issued the "Declaration of Breda," which promised liberty to tender consciences, but the Cavalier Parliament retained control of the nation, and they desired neither Catholic nor Puritan supremacy. Because they wanted civil and religious uniformity, they nullified Charles's pledge to Nonconformists. The 1661 uprising of Fifth Monarchy Men attempting to seize London by force of arms for "King Jesus"—the looked-for messianic fifth monarch—alarmed the government and rendered all sects politically suspect. In May 1662, a specific act was passed against the Quakers. The result: About four thousand "Children of the Light" were rounded up and imprisoned.

The Quaker act continued to stir up a storm of persecution. Fox was rearrested at Swarthmoor Hall. At the hearing he refused to doff his hat, and refused to take the baiting Oath of Supremacy and Allegiance. So he was again committed to prison, as were Margaret Fell and many others. This seventh imprisonment—the longest of Fox's life—began at Lancaster early in 1664 and was completed at Scarborough, in September 1666. Margaret Fell, the gracious gentlewoman who would soon become Fox's wife, actually received a sentence of outlawry under the law of *praemunire*, and lost her possessions. She served four-and-a-half years of a life-long sentence before the king intervened and restored her property. Fox never actually received sentence in open court, but he was treated as if under sentence. When the clerk asked him, in the trial, to "kiss the book," Fox replied wryly but not very diplomatically that because the Book—the Bible—said "Kiss the Son," the book should be imprisoned![14]

At every legal round Fox pointed out errors in his indictment, but the judge would resort to asking for the oath, and in that way keep him under trial. After fourteen months at Lancaster, he was taken to Scarborough Castle and thrown into an open room where the rain swept in and the smoke burned his eyes. While Fox was there, Governor Sir Jordan Crosland came to see him one day. This man was a Roman Catholic and Fox, with his infuriating humor—told him that this was the governor's purgatory into which they had put him.[15]

But Fox bailed the water out of his room, slept in wet clothes, lived on bread and water, and kept his conscience clear! Despite the fact that his body became crippled by rheumatism, his mind stayed keen. His prison cell became his pulpit as he debated opponents who sought him out to test forensic and theatrical skills. Finally the governor must have decided Fox did not belong in this "purgatory," for he became friendly with Fox and secured his release from the king. The officers of the prison said this about their late prisoner: "He was as stiff as a tree, and as pure as a bell." The day after his release, the Great Fire blazed in London. Fox considered this to be God's judgment upon the nation.

The eighth and final imprisonment occurred in a series of "running skirmishes" with the law from 1673-1675. Fox spent about fourteen months in jail. It was during this time that his mother died, deprived of one last visit with her son.

And during this time Fox's health broke, so for a time Friends doubted his recovery. But the Lord had more for Fox to do. He recovered and was freed under Lord Chief Justice Sir Matthew Hale, who quashed the indictment and refused to put the oath to him.

People were brought out of prison by Fox both figuratively and actually. People who came to gawk at the man in the leathern breeches saw the sleazy condition of the jails and the misery that went on within them. Governors and judges and others in authority were made aware that prisoners were human beings. They saw the softening effect of Christian love upon the worst prisoners, as displayed by Fox and his fellows. The Quaker was the thorn in the flesh of careless injustice. He publicized the infamy of holding a person without an accusation. By refusing to take the oaths of either abjuration or allegiance in this era of shifting regimes, he showed England that people of deep religious conscience are her most stalwart citizens, for they do not kowtow to every political wind. While other Englishmen jumped from sworn loyalty to kings to abjuration of monarchy and then back again, Fox played it straight, loyal first to God and then true to his nation and to its citizens. By his refusal to doff the hat, to bribe the jailers, or to "escape" when he was innocently charged, he pricked the conscience of citizens regarding abuses in the English judicial system.

There was a dramatic touch to every courtroom and every jail. As one has written: "He made every courtroom a sounding board for his gospel, every persecution an advertisement of the power of faith."[16]

One of his clever ploys was to address a paper to the court. When asked if it were his, in quixotic humor, he would demand to have it read. In that way the courtroom audience could all hear what he had to say.

Later generations can be thankful for those terrible jail experiences, for out of them came Fox's *Journal* and some of his other writings. It makes no difference whether the literary style of the times seems awkward to us. His words, as though framed by iron bars, with Spirit-driven passion proclaim Christian truth, and lay upon our generation a challenge to be as faithful in the twenty-first century as he and his youthful coworkers were in the seventeenth century.

The sufferings brought success, and with success came the need for guidance and leadership of the thousands of Quakers. To this task George Fox gave himself with considerable insight and organizational skill during the years when he got free from the legal tangles.

TRAVEL
AND
ADMINISTRATION

*"Spare no place, spare no tongue,
nor pen; but be obedient
to the Lord God"*

WHEN HE WAS released from Launceston Castle in 1656, Fox faced two major responsibilities: to expand the movement in aggressive evangelism and to guide its covenant formation. A movement that had started as a prophetic awakening now required administration to keep it together and functioning in unity. Sufferings and the loss of property created a need for organizational structures to care for the believers. Meetings for worship had to be provided for thousands of people disinherited from steeplehouse churches. Then, too, disorders threatened to derail the Quaker ingathering of believers.

Early on, some leaders took advantage of Fox's imprisonment to "do their own thing." James Nayler, a brilliant preacher, is one example. Wanting to dramatize identity with Christ, he paraded down the streets of Bristol one autumn day, accompanied by fanatical followers in a "triumphant entry."[1] What a fiasco!

Despite Nayler's subsequent and genuine repentance, the threat of anarchy loomed. Martin Luther backed down when individuality threatened to morph into anarchy; so he accepted strict state control. Calvin opted for the tight and sometimes cruel rule of the elect as a way to control individual conscience. Fox stressed a faith that the living Christ led people into salvation and guided them together with others throughout life. Fox believed the Scriptures were an outward guide and check, because they were inspired of God, and truth could not lie in opposites. Indeed, the Scriptures could be properly understood only as one knew the Christ of which they spoke. Fox refused to rend the seamless robe of truth. He was firmly convinced that an individual could have God's will as revealed in the written word. Further, Fox believed that the Holy Spirit would *corporately guide* gatherings of people. The church should be free of state control. It should not become a sanctioned monopoly. Lack of unity, Fox thought, arises from disobedience or ignorance of the will of God. Hence each meeting for worship and for business must stress the guidance of the Holy Spirit upon the individual *and* upon the group. He dared to trust individual conscience in its wider applications by harnessing it to the concept of group guidance by the Holy Spirit, workable in so far as a group could be found which listens to the voice of the Spirit.

"In nothing," writes one, "did George Fox show the mark of genius more distinctly than in the way he worked out the organization of his movement and adjusted it to fit his religious ideals."[2]

To support such covenant ideals of church polity, Fox recognized the need for strong, Bible-based preaching. He spent the years 1656-1660 holding large meetings to rally people together in the faith. His personal leadership qualities were amazing, and he lived out his own command:

> Let all nations hear the sound by word or writing. Spare no place, spare no tongue, nor pen; but be obedient to the Lord God: go through the work; be valiant for the truth upon the earth.[3]

When a disturber bothered one of his meetings (as *he* had earlier bothered the meeting in the steeplehouse) where thousands were gathered, Fox let the man speak for a while, after which he charged him "in the dread and power of the Lord to be silent." Then Fox opened the Scriptures to the thousands, some of whom had been hostile. His *Journal* records the procedure and the result:

> For many hours did I declare the word of life amongst them in the eternal power of God; that by him they might come up into the beginning and be reconciled to him. And having turned them to the Spirit of God in themselves, that would lead into all truth, I was moved to pray in the mighty power of God; and the Lord's power came over all....The meeting broke up quietly, and the Lord's power and glory shined over all.[4]

During the first few months following the Launceston imprisonment, Fox held three important "general meetings" in the southern counties for purposes of inspiration, fellowship, and incipient organization. Other such meetings followed in various parts of England. The following year a conference was held at Swarthmoor in which the various leaders met, and arrangements were made for annual meetings at Skipton in Yorkshire. These continued until 1660 and laid the foundation for the organization of the Church. Members of the Friends Church received the nickname "Quaker." The name "Friends" was based upon Jesus' statement "You are my friends if you do what I command" (John 15:14).

The early movement bore various names, such as "Children of Light," "Friends of Truth," or simply "Friends." Not until 1800 did "Society of Friends" come into general use, reflecting its denotation as a legal designation for a non-state church Christian fellowship.

In these meetings arrangements were made to care for the recording of births, deaths, and marriages; to take collections for the poor, the imprisoned, and those who were preaching; and to provide discipline of the disorderly. The marriage ceremony, like the meeting for business, was to be under the leadership of the Holy Spirit, and so recognized by members of the Friends meeting. It must not be just a secular regulation. The legality of this simple pledge of the one party to the other was upheld in Nottingham in 1661, when it was concluded that the consent of the parties makes a marriage.[5] (Quakers were sacramental without being sacerdotal; they believed their commitments conveyed spiritual value without being made sacred by a priest). Whereas Puritans wanted regulation of marriage by the state, the Quakers insisted its covenantal character was best served through oversight by the Christian community (i.e., by the church).

When Fox came "back to life" from his long stay in Lancaster Prison and Scarborough Castle, he found that some people had revolted against any sort of external authority. John Perrot, who had preached widely and suffered under the Inquisition in Rome (until freed because of alleged insanity) went all out against any kind of organization. He even objected to the scheduling of meetings for business or worship; he wanted everything to occur by the *immediate* (meaning spontaneous) guidance of the Spirit. Fox exercised his leadership again, this time with something more permanent than strong preaching and inspirational general meetings. He devised a system of "monthly meetings," composed of several congregations of believers gathered "in the power of God and in the order of the gospel." The next step was the "quarterly meeting," and then the "yearly meeting"—or general meeting as it was first called. Up and down the country, on foot and on horseback, Fox traveled, rallying the members together and explaining the significance of this experience of group business under the guidance of the Holy Spirit. It is a testimony to his administrative ability that many erstwhile Seekers, Ranters, and Familists—known for anarchist tendencies against government and compulsory church rules—rallied about his new discipline of the Spirit.[6]

"Dear Heart. . . "

Fox was now forty-five years of age. The year 1669 brought to him a sense of ease from the relentless pressures that had marked previous years. The Corporation Act (1661), the Act of Uniformity (1662), the Conventicle Act (1664), the Five Mile Act (1665), and the more specific Quaker Act of 1662 had spent their heaviest force. Persecution abated for two reasons. First, the public was absorbed in the devastation of the Great Plague in London (1665), the Great Fire the next year, and the Dutch War (1665-1667). Second, King Charles II increasingly indulged the Nonconformists as a pretext for suspending the penal laws against the Roman Catholics. The first Conventicle Act expired that year.

Some of the ablest members had joined Friends but a short time earlier. Isaac and Mary Penington in 1658, Thomas Ellwood in 1659 (as Milton's secretary, Ellwood urged the writing of *Paradise Regained*, and as a trusted Quaker edited Fox's *Journal*), George Keith in 1663, William Penn and Robert Barclay in 1667-1668. These people brought enthusiasm, scholarship, and influential social standing. They were able to bear much of the brunt of the legal battles that occurred during the times when the Second Conventicle Act was enforced.[7]

With some of the burdens lifted, then, and with a respite from persecutions, George Fox looked again at the gracious hostess of Swarthmoor Hall, Margaret Fell, widowed for the past eleven years. The brief words of the *Journal* tell the beautiful story:

> I had seen from the Lord a considerable time before, that I should take Margaret Fell to be my wife; and when I first mentioned it to her, she felt the answer of Life from God thereunto. But though the Lord had opened this thing to me, yet I had not received a command from Him for the accomplishing of it then. Wherefore I let the thing rest, and went on in the work and service of the Lord, and according as He led me; travelling in this nation, and through Ireland. But now being at Bristol, and finding Margaret Fell there, it opened in me from the Lord that the thing should be accomplished. After we had discoursed the matter together, I told her, "If she also was satisfied with...it now, she should first send for her children.[8]

The daughters and sons-in-law came and George Fox gravely asked them if they had anything against the marriage. All were delighted, and one may suspect that Margaret had been ready for marriage before George. George insisted arrangements be made for all Margaret Fell's property to be willed to the children. He would have no share of it, nor would he provide food for rumor mills that already had been circulating gossip about the two. The marriage took place at Broadmead Meeting House in Bristol, with the seven Fell daughters signing the certificate, and "the Lord joining us together in the honourable marriage," the *Journal* records, "in the everlasting covenant and immortal Seed of life."[9]

There is no doubt but this was one of the highest moments of his life and hers. To one who had denied himself home, comfort, and security on behalf of his Lord, this seemed to be heaven's gift to him. The wealthy, cultured lady and the weaver's son became as one in the Lord. In a sense they symbolized the attraction for the message the Quakers proclaimed—an attraction for people of every social group who desired to walk in simplicity and holiness as zealous and joyous Christians.

About ten days after their marriage, travel and work resumed. His concern was to travel on his preaching tours; hers to minister in the north and care for her family at Swarthmoor. Of settled home life they had little. Margaret Fell writes, "We were willing both of us to live apart some years upon God's account and his truth's service, and to deny ourselves of the comfort which we might have had in being together."[10]

Alas, within weeks of the marriage, persecution renewed and Margaret was jailed. George made efforts to get her released. When George returned from America and was jailed at Worcester, Margaret went to the king to beg *his* release. For two periods of less than two years each, they lived at Swarthmoor together. At other times they were together briefly as they met in various cities. Altogether, in the twenty-one years of their marriage, they spent no more than five years together. Yet love came through, distilled. The daughters and the sons-in-law became as his own children, working with him and honoring him. Through the years of absence from each other, letters traveled back and forth as rapidly as communications would permit. George always addressed Margaret as "Dear Heart." These letters reflect a sober, mature love of two people who find creative, unifying interest in serving the Lord. Here is a sample letter to "Dear Heart":

> To whom is my love, and to the children, in that which changeth not, but is over all; and to all friends in those parts. I have been at Jamaica about five weeks. Friends are generally well; and here is a convincement; but things would be too large to write of. Sufferings in every place attend me; but the blessed Seed is over all: the great Lord

be praised, who is Lord of sea and land, and of all things therein. We intend to pass from hence about the beginning of the next month, toward Maryland, if the Lord please. Dwell all of you in the Seed of God. In His truth I rest in love to you all. (Jamaica, 23rd of the 12th month, 1671.)[11]

"It was upon me from the Lord to go beyond sea."

Before his marriage, Fox had made a trip to Ireland to visit Friends meetings and to strengthen them. After 1671, he toured the far-flung Quaker outposts for nearly twenty years. And as he went he encouraged, reproved, and organized, as well as clarified doctrine against slanders and abuses by diverse opponents. His travel diaries for the American journey are copious. They show the hazards of travel and the dangers of preaching the gospel in the Quaker mode. In company of a number of Friends, Fox sailed for America on a small boat named "Industry." En route to Barbados, the little ship was chased by a Turkish man-of-war. We gain insights into the character of Fox as the captain of the ship Fox was aboard came to Fox for advice! They considered their honored passenger as another Paul. So Fox prayed earnestly and told them not to try to dodge, but to steer on course, and the Lord would take care of them. With the fears of the others allayed, Fox watched from the porthole of his cabin. As the pirate vessel came closer he started to rise, but then he remembered the word of the Lord, that the Lord's life and power was placed between the ships. With that reassurance he went to bed. [12]

Fox endured many hardships on this trip, largely because rheumatism bothered him—a result of his long, cruel imprisonments. But everywhere he went among the American colonies—from Barbados to Jamaica, and along the inland colonies—he saw the harvest of his sowing.

By 1660 the valiant Quakers had established themselves in nearly every colony in the new world. The year 1659 had witnessed the hanging, on Boston Common, of William Robinson and Marmaduke Stephenson. The same fate came to Mary Dyer and William Leddra in years immediately following.

New England Yearly Meeting was established in 1661, holding its annual assembly in Rhode Island. Friends gathered converts among unchurched people from Maine to the Carolinas. Barbados Island became "headquarters," and from this point Fox strengthened the Society and directed the development of the young congregations.

From this New World headquarters Fox wrote his famous "Letter to the Governor of the Barbados." In this letter he clears the Friends of the charges of denying God, Christ Jesus, the Scriptures, and of inciting the Negroes to rebel. It is a clear picture of the doctrinal views which Fox had spoken forth at various times, confirming the fact that the "Publisher of Truth" was not denying the sacrifice and message of Christ, but applying it in all of life, not just in word. He shows how the term *Word* is used for Christ, whereas the term *words of God* denotes the Scriptures. He shows a Christian concern for the Negroes, urging that they not rebel, but that they be taught *as members of a family*, along with Indians and other less-educated people. He warns that masters will be held accountable for these people (some considered that Indians and Negroes had no souls) on the day of judgment when "the Lord Jesus shall be revealed from heaven...taking vengeance on them that know not God, and obey not the gospel or our Lord Jesus Christ."[13]

As Fox toured America he strengthened Friends meetings, preached to the Indians and slept in their villages. He also engaged in a spirited pamphlet debate with Roger Williams ("A New England Fire-Brand Quenched" answered the Baptist leader's diatribe, "A Fox Digged Out of His Burrows"). Finally, Fox envisioned formation of a Quaker colony in America—a dream that William Penn soon fulfilled.

Sailing back to England in 1673, Fox hurried to London for its yearly meeting sessions. His Worcester imprisonment was followed by the two restful years at Swarthmoor, where he completed his *Journal* and prepared for more travels.

In 1677 Fox visited Holland and Germany. His travel is recorded in his diary, and that information, long with testimonies of friends, was included by Ellwood in the editing of the *Journal*. Fox traveled by hired "waggon" to Bremen, and Hamburg, and other cities. He held meetings in Amsterdam, and along with his ministry among Friends he found time to debate theology with Baptists and Jews. William Penn and Robert Barclay joined forces with him on the Continent, adding their scholarly strength to his impassioned apologetics. To places where Fox could not go he wrote epistles. He never hesitated to write his concerns to anyone, high or low. For example, to Johann III, king of Poland, he quoted Eusebius and Irenaeus, early Christian leaders, on behalf of religious liberty for the persecuted Friends at Danzig (Dantzick). He addressed admonitions to many of the rulers of Europe as well as to the "Turk."

After another time of rest and writing at Swarthmoor, Fox toured England. He was about sixty years of age and his body was tired. But he bent his energy to keeping affairs of Friends in order, cheerfully appearing at places where Friends were being persecuted. But no one would touch him. Authorities were wiser now! Nevertheless, many Friends continued to suffer under the Second Conventicle Act.

Fox visited Holland again in 1684, visiting Galenus Abrahams, a Mennonite teacher who had on an earlier visit told

Fox to keep his piercing eyes off of him when he talked. But on this visit they were more congenial, having discovered they held much of the gospel in common.[14]

Finally the long struggles for religious liberty showed promise of the dawning of a new day. Charles II was dead and James II reigned. While Fox was guiding his meetings and directing the evangelization of those who were in the darkness of unbelief and pretended religion, the political forces were beginning to catch up with the dreams of the sufferers. The common rights of Englishmen had been denied the Quakers. But James II pardoned the Nonconformists, and release came for fifteen hundred Quakers then in prison. Of course, this action alarmed the Protestants who feared that such amnesty was an unconstitutional assumption of power intended to pave the way for a Catholic England. But in the "Bloodless Revolution" which followed, William of Orange, a good Protestant, came in. He had made a pledge of toleration and Protestant supremacy. Friends were no longer caught in the vise of political and religious machinations. In 1689 parliament passed the Toleration Act, which gave to Quakers and other Nonconformists a legal place in English life, and gave Friends a limited tolerance.

SIX

PEACE
AND
PROMISE

"All is well..."

AT SIXTY-SEVEN years of age George Fox felt tired. His hardest labor was over; the work of the Lord prospered. Able men and women gave substance to his Pendle Hill vision of a great people to be gathered to the Lord. Yearly meetings had been established and books published. Missionaries proclaimed the gospel in many countries. Knowing that he had not long to live and hoping to heal some quarrels that threatened the unity of the growing Friends movement, Fox wrote a letter to be read after his death. This is what he wrote:

> Keep all your meetings in the name of the Lord Jesus, that be gathered in his name by his light, grace, truth, power and Spirit....In righteousness and holiness dwell....Let no man live to self, but to the Lord, as they will die in him; and seek the peace of the church of Christ....Dwell in the pure, peaceable, heavenly wisdom of God, that is gentle

and easy to be intreated, that is full of mercy; all striving to be of one mind, heart, soul, and judgment in Christ, having his mind and Spirit dwelling in you, building up one another in the love of God, which doth edify the body of Christ, his church, who is the holy head thereof. Glory to God through Christ, in this age and all other ages, who is the Rock and Foundation, the Emmanuel, God with us, Amen, over all, the beginning and the ending.[1]

On January 11, 1691, he preached at Gracechurch Street, London, with "great power and clearness." After he had prayed and the meeting ended, he complained of feeling ill, although he expressed joy at being able to attend the meeting. "I am glad I was here; now I am clear, I am fully clear," he said.[2]

The following day he visited with close friends who came to his bedside. To them he whispered these words, joyous words that matched his radiant face: "All is well: the Seed of God reigns over all, and over death itself."[3]

The next day, Tuesday, January 13, 1691, at 9:30 in the morning he quietly left this life, in peace.

The exact nature of his final illness is not known. No physician seems to have been called nor any medicine taken. The memorial service was held on the following Friday. Four thousand people filled the meetinghouse, courtyard, and passageways at Gracechurch Street to hear and bear testimony to his memory.[4] Ellwood records that the meeting lasted about two hours, "with great and heavenly solemnity, manifestly attended with the Lord's blessed presence and glorious power," after which his body was carried to the Friends burying ground near Bunhill Fields and there committed to the earth. "His memorial shall remain" wrote Ellwood, "and be everlastingly blessed among the righteous."[5]

The headstone carried the initials of name, birthplace, and age of the deceased (sixty-six-and-a-half). Some 66 years later the grave was moved to another spot in the field to allow for building changes. The earlier stone was wantonly destroyed, but a smaller one was set in the wall. In 1876 the present stone was erected. During the 1940-1941 blitz bombings of London, neighboring houses were mostly destroyed but the grave and marker of the preacher of peace in Christ were not disturbed.

As a wise leader Fox had made himself dispensable. No disruptive upheaval followed his death. In the words of historian Braithwaite,

> He had settled authority in the Church upon a basis which gave scope for the gifts of government of all and knew himself to be no hierarch....Indeed, the only succession he had to provide for was that with respect to foreign correspondence...he remained to the last in close touch with affairs, but only as a revered elder among many brethren.[6]

The degree to which the London elders of the "second-day's meeting" answered their correspondents from other parts of the world "in the wisdom of God" has been variously assessed. For all of the vicissitudes of the religious life that followed through the Quaker movement in the decades and centuries to follow, one may be assured that those who picked up the mantle of the fallen prophet were caught, as he was, by an impelling vision of the greatness of Jesus Christ who offers salvation to all who come to God in faith and gathers redeemed people from every tribe and tongue and people and nation into a covenant of peace.

over the head of the liar" and "nothing may reign but the truth."[4] The law is to be honored, even if one must suffer the consequences of disobeying it for conscience sake; for only in this manner are injustices pictured against a backdrop of truth.

George Fox considered the payment of taxes to be a consistent practice. He wrote:

> And as for the rulers, that are to keep peace, for peace's sake, and the advantage of truth, give them their tribute. But to bear and carry carnal weapons to fight with, the men of peace...they cannot act in such things under the several powers; but have paid their tribute.[5]

This sort of Christian faith is admittedly rugged: It cannot be sustained by unaided human will. To cut loose from the apron strings of princes or parliaments, to request freedom to evangelize for the faith without special privilege and in free competition with other ideologies requires one to have great confidence in one's source of spiritual strength, and also in the nature of the truth one proclaims.

Fox POSSESSED such confidence, borne of quiet prayer. Heaven and earth were conjoined with him because he labored so constantly in prayer. William Penn recognized this quality of devotional life, for in the introduction of Fox's *Journal* he lifted up this tribute: "Above all he excelled in prayer."

Sometimes George Fox sat in silent prayer before an expectant audience and "famished them for words." The listeners sensed that here was one who talked with God and God talked with him. Melted by conviction for their own "distance from God," they responded earnestly to the evangelistic appeal. Prayer, more than rhetoric, empowered his words. Although there are literary gems of spiritual insight tucked into pages of awkward prose, his writing is not consistently powerful. The sheer magnetism of a victorious soul, however, empowers the words and tugs at the heart of any serious reader.

So it was with the spoken word. He reached beyond words to people's souls, conveying the "sure word of prophecy" he had discovered and for which they longed. Fox was the man with a confident word from God in his day. Groups of spiritually hungry folks, disillusioned by the stones which formal religion offered them instead of bread, gathered to hear one who spoke with Spirit-filled assurance. The Seekers, as these groups are sometimes called, were characterized by a contemporary, John Jackson, "as sheep unfolded, and as soldiers unrallied, waiting for a time of gathering."[6]

Another contemporary, John Saltmarsh, said "they wait for an apostle or some one with a visible glory and power able in the spirit to give *visible demonstration of being sent.*"[7] (What a phrase! Would to God that it might be said about more Christians today, Quakers included, that they "give visible demonstration of being sent.") Like a Moses in close communion with the Lord, Fox gave leadership to these spiritually "displaced-persons" and led them into a promised land of victorious Christian faith, sheltered, not in the caves of individualism, but within the fellowship of the church of the redeemed, the "enfolded sheep of God."

The Puritan epic of salvation included introspection as a method by which a properly anxious wayfarer might witness divine stirrings within and thus find assurance of eternal election. Fox arose from a position of an uncertain supplicant to one whose calling and election have been assured by faith "in Christ." Hence his prayer reflected the confidence of one who, like Abraham, has become a "friend of God"—an heir of God and joint-heir with Christ—to whom God deigns to reveal his will and work. To his detractors this assurance of divine approval constituted unwarranted "enthusiasm." But to his followers it was a recovered gospel order for all who would be filled with the Spirit of God.

The creative spiritual leader who bequeathed his boots to Thomas Lower left a legacy larger than an example of dynamic Christian leadership. He left his followers strong teachings about two important biblical teachings: the doctrine of holiness and the church as a covenant community.

THE DOCTRINE OF HOLINESS

The doctrine of holiness Fox lifted boldly from Scripture and offered to those who dared to walk without crutches of priesthood, ritual, or state-religion. The prevailing theological winds of Fox's England were from an icy north. So bound was man to sin, taught most ministers then, that he could never get clear from the meshes of sin. True, in the counsels of divine election certain ones might be forgiven by the grace of God, but they remained sinners whose multiform transgressions were obscured from the sight of an offended God by the Christ, the sacrificial offering. This was hyper-Calvinism. In purer forms the Reformed theology had sought to elevate the sovereignty of God to prevent man's arrogant assumption of merited or earned salvation. But the finer nuances of Calvinist theology got lost in popularized versions. They turned salvation into a sort of legal transaction whereby heaven might be populated without divine loss of face. Thomas Loe (the preacher whose ministry brought William Penn to the Lord) made the comparison succinctly: "There is a faith which overcomes the world, and there is a faith which is overcome by the world."[8]

Victimized alike by human cupidity and exigencies of politico-religious strife, Calvinism had become a faith overcome by the world of selfish greed: priest and parishioner alike didn't know the living Christ experientially. In reaction, the radical edge of Puritanism became convinced that the Reformation—so ably brought to Europe by Luther and Calvin—"had settled for less," and with its over-emphasis upon justification by faith had not made proper allowance for the *fruits* of righteousness. In seeking to steer clear of monastic forms of holiness it had cut off the most vital aspect of Christian experience, not allowing for inward purity and outward morality. The Quakers refused to consider as adequate a practice arising from Anabaptism, of rejecting the efficacy of infant baptism and replacing it with adult baptism; they sought Spirit baptism through which a forgiven sinner finds moral and spiritual purification of heart and life.

The particular spiritual experiences of Fox have been stated in earlier chapters of this book. He had witnessed salvation from sin; he had been plunged into an empathetic sense of the sinfulness of human nature. And then he had come to know with full assurance a state of pureness, innocence, and righteousness. He had suffered imprisonment for blasphemy because he claimed he was sanctified and that Christ had taken away his sin.

Although George Fox was the driving force in early Quakerism, he was not a systematic theologian. He did not arrange in logical arrangement the principles he proclaimed. Yet his doctrinal formulations are not inferior to those of Barclay or Penn. Fox was, after all, the Bible-trained and Spirit-led instrument of the Quaker Awakening. From his stern condemnation of sinner-Christianity and his gentle pleadings for a life of holiness and purity, Barclay and Penn received their instruction. Out of living experience Fox wrote, checking and supporting his many pamphlets and doctrinal works with Scripture. Central to his thought and normative for the whole Quaker movement is the concept of Christian perfection—of a victory over sin in this life. R. Newton Flew declares that "in religious and ethical insight, George Fox went far deeper than the Reformers, and he did so precisely in virtue of his teaching on perfection."[9]

What is the purpose for the light of Christ that "lighteth every man"? That people might be drawn back through the flaming sword, "to the second Adam," from the first Adam to have sins and transgressions blotted out.[10]

In blunt language Fox charged that doctrines claiming "people must be in sin while they be upon the earth" nullifies the sacrifice of Christ. In effect it will "make Christ's dying in vain, and the one offering of no value, which hath perfected for ever all them that are sanctified, and his blood of none effect, which cleanseth from all sin."[11]

The Holy Spirit "plunges down" the old nature, he said, and brings to the one head, Christ, through whose sacrifice men come to know the awfulness of their sin, are pardoned, and made just. Men may continue in the assurance of salvation because Christ within is able to save to the uttermost and to keep those who commit their way to him.[12]

Discoursing on Romans, Fox writes,

And this we witness who are in scorn called Quakers, but Christ did not die for sinners that they should live all their lifetime in sin, and die in their sins; but that as sin had reigned unto death, so grace might also reign through righteousness unto eternal life.[13]

Against all nominal Christians he addressed these pointed words:

> And all ye letter-professors that plead for Imperfection, and your body of sin and death to the grave, which are the devil's dregs, these gates (the New Jerusalem) are guarded against you with that great luggage on your backs to enter in at.[14]

George Fox's meaning is clear and unclouded! One cannot reach heaven dragging along a sinful nature.

He insisted upon this, however: Such perfection was made possible *only* through Christ. Here is no pantheistic perfection, no absorption into the infinite. The mysticism of Fox certainly adheres to Christ's redemption and to the mystery of that fellowship. "He sees life as black and white; there are no grey shades,"[15] is one characterization of his view.

Such prophetic perfectionism is Christ-centered. "That which purges this [carnal nature] out of him is the blood of Christ, who by his blood and fiery baptism hath purged out our sins, and sanctifies us." Those who plead for purgatorial purging (the Roman Catholics, or "Papists" as they were known) and those who plead for perfection at the grave (Calvinists) are blind as the Jews, averred Fox, and are ignorant of the Sanctifier. Indeed, they are the "Devil's teachers," not Christian teachers.[16]

Flew attests to this Christo-centricity focus in these words: "The chief distinction of the Quaker doctrine of perfection was that its centre was in the Cross of Christ."[17]

Man is enlightened that he may be restored to the image of God, that he may come "to the second Adam, from the first Adam," to have his sins and transgressions blotted out. "The church in God...are they who are born again of the immortal seed, by the word of God...which word became flesh, and dwelt among us; so he (Christ) is the head of the church, and they are lively stones."[18]

Fox shared the Puritan view of human depravity to the extent that he believed that without God's grace no one could be saved. He discovered evil to be the basic thing to be conquered and found its fortress in the heart. This nature is variously described as "the body of sin and death," the "devil's dregs," the "devil's works," "imperfection," "the bad, cursed state," "the fallen estate," and "the state of Adam in the fall." In such a doctrine of original sin, arbitrary election and imputed righteousness are cast aside as unworthy. They are replaced by election in Christ and imparted righteousness. This impartation is the infusion of a new principle of life in the believer. A "fall" which is morally significant can be answered only by a restoration likewise morally significant. Only then comes real atonement. If there were no sanctifying power in the atonement anyone might *claim* to be a Christian, asserted Fox. Such a one is a "vain man in a dead faith" who knows no victory over the conditions of depravity.[19] For individuals so transformed, however, Christ is the *real presence,* giving individual leadership and corporate direction. This does not lead to infallibility of judgment—people are still human—nor to magic, for inspiration is united to redemptive history and to the will of God as revealed in Scripture. Puritan "wayfaring and warfaring" had for him a destination and a victory in *this* life as well as in the next. The battle was turned without and not fought throughout life within. "And now, glory be to the Lord for ever," he exulted, "thousands of these way-faring men are come to find their way, Christ Jesus."[20]

Throughout his ministry, Fox insisted that such imparted holiness is demonstrable. It would be illogical to assume anything else. An admonition given in 1662 reflects his earnest desire to see people continue in, and grow in holiness. These words are no lazy musings of a pipe-dreamer; rather they are golden words, melted in the crucible of persecution:

> All keep to the beauty of holiness; for in holiness lies your beauty; and the fruits of righteousness is a tree of life, and the name of the Lord is a strong tower, and the righteous flee into it, and are safe.[21]

To summarize: Fox held that perfection, or life above sin, is possible in this life, that the "body of death" which is destroyed is original sin, the Adamic nature. He asserted that this sinful nature is destroyed, purged, or cleansed from the heart by Christ's baptism with the Holy Spirit. Such is the purpose of the atonement, making the outward sacrifice of Christ meaningful inwardly as a result of God's grace and man's faith. *Justification is considered completed in sanctification.* Fox speaks of one work of grace, contrary to popular terminology often employed because of the influence of the contemporary Wesleyan holiness movement. ("And justification and sanctification are one...not two things really distinct in their nature, but really one.")[22] The experiences of Fox and others show how this grace is received by steps, or crises, until a completed work of cleansing and blessed assurance of victory. Fox, by linking together these aspects of regeneration, made it clear that sanctification is not an accessory at extra cost for elite Christians, but is part and parcel of the experience for every true Christian believer.

Finally, the experience of sanctification and the life of holiness are integrally related—the one is the fruit of the other, and all is by the virtue and power of Christ. Such a heritage has been a rather difficult burden for Friends to carry through the centuries. To be over-sensitive ethically

and under-sensitive emotionally, or over-sensitive emotionally and under-sensitive ethically have been constant perils.
Other early Friends shared this vision of holiness, too, as the
following examples indicate.

ISAAC PENINGTON, a scholarly leader among the
Independents, came into contact with Quakers in 1658.
Wrote he of his heart-hunger:

> My soul was not satisfied with what I met with, nor indeed
> could be, there being further quickenings and pressings in
> my spirit after a more full, certain and satisfactory
> knowledge...for I saw plainly that there was a stop of the
> streams, and a great falling short of the power, life, and
> glory which they partook of. We had not so the Spirit, nor
> were so in the faith, nor did so walk and live in God as they
> did.[23]

Coming into a meeting of Friends, and feeling the presence and power of God among them, he knew the Spirit to be
speaking to his heart. Here's the sequel:

> Yea, I did not only feel words and demonstrations from
> without, but I felt the dead quickened, the seed raised;
> insomuch that my heart...said, This is He, this is He, there
> is no other: this is He whom I have waited for and sought
> after from my childhood; who was always near me, and
> had often begotten life in my heart; but I knew him not
> distinctly, nor how to receive him, or dwell with him. And
> then, in this sense, in the melting and breakings of my
> spirit, was I given up to the Lord, to become his, both in
> waiting for the further revealing of his seed in me, and to
> serve him in the life and power of his seed.[24]

Concluding his personal testimony, Penington states, "I
have met with the true peace, the true righteousness, the true
holiness, the true rest of the soul, which the redeemed dwell
in."[25]

Concerning complete sanctification, he wrote:

> But there is a power in Christ to perfect the work of redemption in the heart; to sanctify the creature wholly, in body, soul, and spirit; yea, his leaven received will work and works daily, till it hath wrought all out, and the whole be leavened; and he that truly feeleth it so, can say in God's presence, and in the true fear and humility of heart, the old leaven is wholly wrought out, and the new hath wholly leavened me; this is not the voice of deceit, but of truth in him.[26]

One gathers from this that Penington viewed sanctification as progressive until a time came when complete victory was effected. Here is a fine selection from Penington, one whom Friends honor as a deeply contemplative man—a gentle, mystic soul.

> Will God dwell in an unholy temple? Will he dwell where sin dwells? He may indeed to such, when at any time they are tender, and truly melted before him, be to them as a wayfaring man that tarries for a night; but he will not take up his abode there, walk there, sup there, and give them to sup with him.[27]

Penington insists that within the life of holiness much daily must be learned of Christ. New knowledge to supplant ignorance, enlightening the eyes to behold wondrous things out of God's love—such is the path of perfection for Penington. On this path no one becomes static, confusing perfection with permanence or holiness with hardness. It is a highway of love for God and for man. He adds:

> And as he dies to himself, Christ will reveal himself more and more in him, and he shall feel the pure seed of life springing more and more up in him, and living in him, and he in it; in and through which he shall come more and

more into union and fellowship with the Father of spirits, and the whole living body of his church and people.[28]

William Penn claimed the victorious Christian experience after listening to preaching by Thomas Loe. His choice for Christ was attended by real sacrifice. Like Moses he chose to suffer affliction with the children of God rather than to enjoy the pleasures of sin for a season. The elder Penn had protested angrily when William joined the "despised" sect. But within a year this cultured young man was preaching with Quakers and suffering the bitter fruits of his labor—namely, imprisonment. Locked up in the London Tower on charges of blasphemy he wrote an evocative treatise, *No Cross, No Crown*. As a modern rich young ruler who accepted the challenge of Christ, he found no sorrow from this relationship, but rather joy. Hear his words from prison:

> O come! Let us follow Him, the most unwearied, the most victorious captain of our salvation; to whom all the great Alexanders and mighty Caesars of the world are less than the poorest soldier of their camps could be to them. True, they were all great princes of their kind, and conquerors too, but on very different principles. For Christ made himself of no reputation, to save mankind; but these plentifully ruined people to augment theirs. They vanquished others, not themselves; Christ conquered self, that ever vanquished them; of verity therefore the most excellent Prince and Conqueror. Besides, they advanced their empire by rapine and blood, but He by suffering and persuasion; He never by compulsion, they always by force prevailed. Misery and slavery followed all their victories, his brought greater freedom and felicity to those he overcame. In all they did they sought to please themselves; in all he did he aimed to please his Father, who is King of kings and Lord of lords. It is this most perfect pattern of self-denial we must follow, if ever we will come to glory.

And ponder Penn' s closing prayer:

O Lord God, thou lovest holiness, and purity is thy delight in the earth; wherefore I pray thee, make an end of sin and finish transgression, and bring in thy everlasting righteousness to the souls of men, that thy poor creation may be delivered from the bondage it groans under, and the earth enjoy her sabbath again: that thy great name may be lifted up in all nations, and thy salvation renowned to the ends of the world. For thine is the kingdom, the power, and the glory, forever. Amen.[29]

William Penn is remembered for attempts to hew out a Christian colony in the New World. His fair dealings with Indians were remarkable in an era of cruel exploitation. His contact with tribal Indians is supposed to be the only treaty never ratified by an oath and never broken. To this day Quakers have had a peculiar responsibility to the Native Americans, for a time in an administrative capacity under the government's direction, and in this century, in mission and relief work in various places, including Oklahoma and southern Oregon. The political efforts of Penn were not longlasting, at least directly, but they demonstrated on the ground how Christian conscience sustains good governance.

Penn's character is first shown by the willingness of this prominent man to join the despised Quakers. His ideals stemmed from his experience of Christ, and not from human aspirations, and they succeeded in proportion to the faith and practice of Christian principles which people were willing to display. Through Penn, and through others for whom he stands as an example, Quakers have been reputed to be generous, caring people, demonstrating integrity in private and public service. *Compassion* has become a watchword by which Quakers are known. What is often forgotten (and sometimes by Quakers themselves) is the spiritual base for

brought out of natural depravity (the Adamic nature). The response is possible from *all* people, not just from the elect, for it is Christ who enlightens. Humankind does not have a "divine spark" which is "theirs" simply because they are humans—salvation would then be by his own effort—but humankind is *enlightened by Christ,* the divine Word who became flesh and was crucified for the sins of the world. To everyone, living on a plane of unrighteousness, unable to respond to God, Christ gives light. This universal and saving light brings the responsive one to a place of repentance. Then the redemption wrought by Christ "without us" (i.e., at Jerusalem), becomes a particular redemption bringing justification "within us." This justification first pardons and then makes pure. And so the body of sin is displaced; one is brought to a plane of holiness, to tread upward rejoicing in the love of Christ. Perfect obedience enlarges the sphere of responsible love toward God and toward one's fellows.[36]

O BSERVE NOW the testimony of some other young people who found vital Christian experience through the ministry of Fox and other Quaker leaders. William Caton, a prayerful, earnest youth of seventeen, testified thus:

> The power of the Lord God did work mightily and effectually in me to the cleansing, purging, and sanctifying of me....And then I began to be broken, melted and overcome with the love of God which sprung in my heart, and the Divine and precious promises that were confirmed to my soul.[37]

This teenaged convert engaged in missionary service and died from hardship and abuse at the age of twenty-nine.

John Audland, an Independent preacher, listened in 1652 to Fox declare the present portion for believers to know the indwelling Christ, to know that "their bodies might be prepared, sanctified, and made fit temples for God and Christ to dwell in." It touched his heart.[38]

Francis Howgill heard the same three-hour sermon at Firbank Fell. Sewell writes of Howgill:

> But although he, who had been trained up in the university to be a minister, became a teacher amongst the Independents, and was zealous in virtue; yet he remained dissatisfied in himself, finding that notwithstanding all his fasting, praying, and good works, the root of sin still remained in him; and although the common doctrine was that Christ had taken the guilt of sin upon himself, yet this could not satisfy him; because his conscience told him, "His servant thou art, whom thou obeyest."[39]

Edward Burrough came in touch with Fox, through whose ministry Burrough experienced a "fiery baptism." He became one of the most faithful and able preachers of that generation. "Praised be the Lord for evermore," he declared, "who made me partaker of His love, in whom my soul hath full satisfaction, joy and content."[40]

William Dewsbury struggled with the desire to be free from sin. Note the sensitivity of spirit shown in these words:

> And by the power of this Word I was armed with patience to wait in His counsel; groaning under the body of sin in the day and hour of temptation, until it pleased the Lord to manifest His power to free me, which was in the year 1651.[41]

John Crook heard a voice from heaven telling him plainly that:

> whatever the Lord would communicate and make known of Himself and the mysteries of His kingdom, He would do it in a way of purity and holiness. I saw then such a brightness in holiness, and such a beauty in an upright and pure righteous conversation and close circumspect waking

with God in a holy life...that it sprang freely in me, that all religion and all profession without it were as nothing in comparison with this communion.[42]

Falling away into disobedience, Crook hungered to know freedom over sin. Under the preaching of Dewsbury he attained his desire, that of "walking with God in holiness and purity."

Stephen Crisp heard of the Quakers teaching that sin might be overcome in this life, and for this he longed. After James Parnell had preached in Colchester in 1655, Crisp could record these words:

> And the cross was laid upon me, and I bore it; and as I became willing to take it up I found it to be to me that thing which I had sought from my childhood, even the power of God.[43]

He became one of the most influential of the early Quaker ministers.

Thomas Story was a poet. In 1689 he experienced a wonderful conversion. Here is his testimony:

> Now all my past sins were pardoned and done away, and my carnal reasonings and conceivings about the knowledge of God and the mysteries of religion were over....I now found the true Sabbath, a holy, heavenly, divine, and free rest, and the most sweet repose!

Story records this complete victory which came as he committed his cause to the Savior:

> From about eight in the evening till midnight the eye of my mind was fixed on the love of God, which still remained sensible in me, my soul cleaving thereto with great simplicity, humility, and trust therein, without any yielding to Satan and his reasonings on those subjects where flesh and blood, in its own strength, is easily overcome. But

about twelve at night the Lord put him to utter silence with all his temptations for that season, and the life of the Son of God alone remained in my soul. And then, from a sense of his wonderful work and redeeming love, this saying of the Apostle arose in me with power. "The Law of the spirit of life in Christ Jesus hath made me free from the law of sin and death."[44]

Such are the testimonies of some seventeenth century Quaker leaders. They reflect individuality of expression and training, but reveal similar yearnings for and responses to God. They all longed for purity of heart; they all attest that the human heart can be made pure.

Proclamation of holiness is tested outwardly by actions produced and evidence of virtuous life. The love and loyalty of early Friends met these tests. Critics said, "Look how the Quakers love and take care of one another."[45] Purity of heart expressed itself in kindness and sympathy; and this tenderness toward the sufferings of others marks the Quaker witness. Friends offered to stay in stinking jails for one another. They showed a surprising amount of restorative compassion to leaders who messed up.

As noted earlier, one misguided Quaker leader, James Nayler, had carried the idea of union with Christ too far with his "triumphant entry" into Bristol. This foolish scenario brought reproach to already beleaguered Quakers. The leaders, while sternly repudiating his act, dealt with him kindly. Remorseful and penitent, Nayler suffered horrible civil punishment for his "crime"—whipped for two hours, tongue bored with a hot iron, forehead branded with the letter *B* for blasphemy, whipped again, and imprisoned at hard labor. Partly because of "the spirit of meekness" which characterized his fellow-Quakers, he returned to a firm faith in God before his battered body gave out. Shortly before he died from this terrible abuse, Nayler penned these poignant lines: "There is a spirit which I feel, that delights to do no evil...its crown is meekness, its life is everlasting love unfeigned."[46]

Of the joy with which Friends received him back an early writer testifies, "I do esteem it a particular mark of God's owning his people, in bringing back into unity with them, a man who had so dangerously fallen, as did James Nayler."[47]

THE PRACTICE OF HOLY LIVING extended beyond the borders of the fellowship of believers. For George Fox pacifism was part of the life of holiness. He argued and preached peace from doctrinal reasons, not just from political or social concerns. His first concern was for heart purity; peace followed as the consistent fruit of the new nature. Of one belligerent fellow who threatened his life, Fox said:

> I went to him and was moved in the power of the Lord to speak to him. I told him, the Law said, "An eye for an eye, and a tooth for a tooth," but thou threatenest to "kill all the Quakers, though they have done thee no hurt." But, said I, here is gospel for thee: "Here's my hair, here's my cheek, here's my shoulder," turning it to him. This came so over him, that he and his companions stood as men amazed, and said, "If that was our principle, and if we were as we said, they never saw the like in their lives. I told them, "What I was in words, I was the same in life."[48]

The Quakers took seriously the teaching of James that war comes from the lust of the heart; hence for the one who is sanctified and purified, in whom the devil and his works is destroyed, carnal warfare is out of the question. Fox wrote

> Ye are called to peace, therefore follow it; that peace is in Christ, not in Adam in the fall. All that pretend to fight for Christ are deceived; for his kingdom is not of this world,

therefore his servants do not fight. Fighters are not of Christ's kingdom, but are without...for his kingdom stands in peace and righteousness, but fighters are in the lust: and all that would destroy men's lives are not of Christ's mind, who came to save men's lives.[49]

Of the seventeenth century Quakers one writer declared "They therefore bore an unwavering testimony against war in all its varied phases...seeking a kingdom not of this world, they could no longer fight."[50]

This part of the Quaker heritage has been often misunderstood. Sometimes it has been misused and distorted. It has not been as "unwavering" among later Friends as it was for the early Friends, although it stands yet as one of the marks of the movement and is adhered to by the many members. The holiness-pacifist manifesto sounds strange to many Christians currently. Common opinion says pacifism belongs to liberal Christianity and that the nonpacifist position belongs to the more orthodox or fundamentalist ones. Polarizing the holiness-pacifist doctrine of early Quakers occurred during the early twentieth century largely as a result of the modernist-fundamentalist rift which divided Protestant Christianity, dealing out ethics to modernists and personal salvation to fundamentalists, both supported by selective biblical interpretation. The earlier evangelicals, however, would not have considered an evangelically-based pacifism an anomaly: Dwight L. Moody, the great nineteenth-century evangelist, and G. Campbell Morgan, brilliant Bible expositor, were pacifists, as their biographies and writings attest.[51]

Although this is not the place for an extended discourse on the peace testimony of Friends throughout the years, one observation is germane: Whenever the doctrine of complete victory over sin has been minimized or denied, the political and social aspects of peace begin to predominate, after which the pacifist position drifts toward relativism—lacking the compelling power of Spirit-driven conviction—so that Quakers either will not pay the social price for a pacifist stand or they seek to justify this heritage on pragmatic grounds. This eventually leads into logical dead ends, dilemmas, and eventually to disillusion. Despite failures, however, the Friends peace testimony—in concert with those of other historic peace churches such as the Brethren and Mennonite—has enriched the world. Individual Christians from many denominations now share the vision. The Quaker leaven has sensitized the conscience of the church and forced a re-examination of just-war theories and social justice in the light of biblical teachings. The belligerent idealism of World War I was not found among the churches during World War II, at least, not in as great a measure as before. The notion of a holy war receded further during the remaining years of that bloody century. At mid-twentieth century, the optimistic hope that Christian theology would more widely embrace both heart holiness and pacifism was subsequently dashed by powerful forces of political militancy—imperial and insurgent—by antinomian reactions to legalistic holiness teachings, and by cultural pressures for relativistic ethics.

In addition to the pacifist position, the doctrine of complete atonement in Christ led the early Quakers to certain "peculiar" testimonies—scruples that seem rather trivial to the modern mind, but that embodied principles of integrity. For example, early Friends refused to give the oath in court in deference to the biblical injunction, "Swear not at all" (see Matthew 5:36). To those in whom the very living Christ dwells there is but one standard: truth always. The taking of oaths implies a double standard of truth. It impugns the veracity of a Christian and casts aspersion on the atoning Christ to ask a believer to *swear* to tell the truth. As a concession to a religious scruple, several governments allow the affirmation in lieu of the oath. But beyond a particular concession, the Quaker legacy is this: reverence for truth. The whole Christian church, and indeed society as molded by principles of trust, has been the beneficiary of this legacy. In a secular world shaken by the winds of pragmatism (facts, not "truth" are important) this witness to the inviolate character of truth and its obligations upon the children of God has been a steadying force within the Christian community.

In similar ways, refusal to doff the hat to people of high station (an extravagance of the times) signified their rejection of artificiality in social conventions. Reverence belongs to God alone, and all kinds of bowing and scraping before human leaders or celebrities smacks of the idolatrous. This explains their abhorrence of titles and other extravagant social amenities and their use of the simple language for all. While simplicity of dress became a fad in later years (Quaker gray), in the early times Friends dressed according to custom, sans fancy trimmings. They reflected the soberness of their Puritan environment. This testimony was certainly overdone by an austere dress code that characterized the second wave of the Quaker movement. Margaret Fell saw a creeping legalism in this rigorous attitude. She loved red cloth and deplored as a "silly gospel" the increasing emphasis upon severity of dress. This second wave of Quakers offers a historic warning to any who in a zeal for holiness seek an easy identification by a badge of dress or demeanor. It may well be concluded that relegation of moral issues to the trivial, for the sake of an assumed inner discipline, marks loss of courage to apply the holiness message in larger areas of evangelism and ethics.

The Quaker movement, despite its failures, remains a valiant attempt to make holiness normative for all Christians and for all social situations. The vagaries of the movement have modified the perfectionist doctrines—sometimes losing, sometimes distorting, but still following after the one who said of the Holy Spirit, "He that is with you shall be in you." This legacy has enriched the entire church. The bold assertion of victorious living, by the seventeenth century Quakers, remains a challenge not only to Friends, but to other Christians as well. The quiet witness of eighteenth century Friends, who "centered down" deep in the mystical life with Christ, differs from the turbulence of the pioneers. These second-century followers sought to bring every thought and intent into subjection to the light of Christ. Their journals are full of introspection. Plain dress, plain speech, close fellowship, colonization, retreat from the trappings of the world—such were the ways of their witness. Modern Quakers are prone to lament the loss of nerve which seemed to draw their forefathers from evangelistic zeal to ethical scrupulosity, from aggressive spiritual warfare against the ungodly to punctilious preoccupation with the "testimonies" and in-group marriages. Yet from such separatism came deep spiritual insights which bore the witness of holiness to the world, perhaps in spite of their oddness, perhaps because of the discipline which such standards necessitated.

John Woolman is the outstanding example from that second century. From the strength of this man's tender conscience issued a growing and insistent conviction in America that slavery was sinful. The leaven of his concern worked to free Friends from their slaves, and then to quicken the hearts of other Christians in the land. It was not just that he opposed slavery; he opposed it with the force of love for slave *and* slaveholder, a force that melted hearts and opened way for the spirit of Christ to effect change. Woolman grieved over wrong and made the sufferings of it his own. "As death comes on our own wills and a new life is formed in us," he mused in his *Journal*, "the heart is purified and prepared to understand clearly, 'Blessed are the pure in heart, for they shall see God.' In purity of heart the mind is divinely opened to behold the nature of universal righteousness, or the righteousness of the kingdom of God."[52]

THE NINETEENTH-CENTURY EXPRESSION of the holiness legacy of Fox reached its highest form in the Richmond Declaration of Faith of 1887. The significance of this document may be gained by sketching events leading up to its formulation. The Hicksite-Gurney divisions of the early decades of the century provided sad evidence of a Church that had so depended upon immediacy of religious experience, unchecked by scriptural revelation, that it succumbed to winds of rationalism, Unitarianism, and subjectivism. Religious experience and exhortation lost mooring in the historical events of Jesus' life, death, and resurrection. *Christ within* became for some only a term for inner feelings. Joseph John Gurney contributed much to the revitalizing of the Society of Friends and its subsequent outreach in evangelism, education, missions, and the establishment of new meetings throughout frontier America. This English Friend emphasized the use of Scripture and teaching methods. He formulated doctrinal statements in lucid terms, thus bringing Friends back to historic Christianity. He sought to maintain a fine balance in the doctrine of atonement in Christ by equal stress upon justification (which he used in a more restricted sense than the seventeenth century Quakers) and sanctification. His memoirs relate this view concerning the atonement provided by God's sacrifice of his son Jesus Christ:

> I believe that God hath appointed this sacrifice...as a means of atonement....This pardoning of sinners, for Christ's sake, is what I understand by the term "justification."

> In order to partake of these mercies, I must possess a living faith, which shall lead me, first, to place my whole hope of acceptance with God in the merits of my Redeemer; and, secondly, to obey the dictates of the Holy Spirit, whom Christ has sent to bring me to repentance, to purge me from all sin, and to guide me in the way to life eternal. This work of the Spirit, by which we become freed from sin, born again, new creatures, is what I understand by the term "sanctification."

> These two, justification and sanctification, I believe to be necessary and sufficient for the salvation of my soul—the first, the cause—the second the condition; both the result of the grace of God, in Christ Jesus my Lord.[53]

People's part is to receive the grace of God by *faith*—for the forgiveness of sins and for drawing down onto the believer "the sanctifying graces of the Holy Spirit—and by *obedience,* which constitutes righteousness and enables Christians to perfect holiness in the fear of God.[54]

The Gurneyite emphasis upon the process of sanctification within the limits of obedience avoided dangers of a static concept of holiness experience and also proclaimed victory over the principle of sin. In some ways his views mediate between "suppressionist" and "eradicationist" positions on sanctification.

A similar position among Irish Friends may be noted by reference to the 1841 *Discipline,* which states this about Jesus Christ, "It is through Him whom God hath set forth to be a propitiation, through faith in his blood, that we obtain pardon for sin; and it is through the power of his Spirit working mightily in us, that we come eventually to experience freedom from sin."[55]

In the liberating spirit of Gurney, American Quakers adapted to demands of their vast country, catching the fire of revival from the Methodists. A largely-attended youth meeting in 1860, during sessions of Indiana Yearly Meeting, ignited revival fires among Friends nationwide. Through these revivals came new modes of worship: singing, organs, use of the mourners' bench and the altar of prayer, and the pastoral system. Conservatives were shocked, but the innovations, refined through the years, have remained, to the enlargement and purification of the Quaker movement. Today a majority of Friends around the world belong to "pastoral" meetings—a fact often ignored by public stereotypes of the Quaker, and more sadly by historians who ought to know better.[56]

The revivals of the post-Civil War period did, however, provoke doctrinal rethinking, particularly when Ohio Yearly Meeting began to make concessions of water baptism. In fact, dissension produced by these departures from Quaker practice led to a significant conference at Richmond, Indiana, in 1887. Friends sensed a need for doctrinal clarity amid the emotional ferment of revival, and a need to instruct those swept into churches by revival, who were ignorant of Quaker teachings. The holiness message as preached by revivalists and teachers such as David B. Updegraff, William Pinkham, John Henry Douglas, and Dougan Clark laid heavy stress upon the *crisis* experience of sanctification, preaching it in terms of a second definite work of grace to be sought by believers and received instantaneously. This holiness emphasis constituted a "rightist" reaction against Quietism and a hedge against an already-threatening modernism. Although revivalist terminology differed from older formulations, especially concerning such terms as *work of grace* and *justification*, it held much in common with Barclay, Penn, and Fox. All agreed that holiness is a realizable goal in this life through the atonement offered in Christ. (Recall that Fox had been clapped into jail because he dared claim—with audacity unmatched by Wesley—that he was sanctified).

THE RICHMOND DECLARATION OF FAITH, which arose from these concerns to recenter Quaker teachings, was largely the work of J. Bevan Braithwaite of London, James E. Rhoads of Philadelphia, and James Carey Thomas of Baltimore. It remains one of the major Quaker formulations of doctrine to this day. An excerpt concerning sanctification reads:

> Sanctification is experienced in the acceptance of Christ in living faith for justification, in so far as the pardoned sinner through faith in Christ is clothed with a measure of His righteousness and receives the Spirit of promise....We rejoice to believe that the provisions of God's grace are sufficient to deliver from the power as well as from the guilt, of sin, and to enable His believing children always to triumph in Christ....Whosoever submits himself wholly to God, believing and appropriating His promises, and exercising faith in Christ Jesus, will have his heart continually cleansed from all sin, by his precious blood,

and through the renewing, refining power of the Holy Spirit, be kept in conformity to the will of God, will love Him with all his heart, mind, soul and strength, and be able to say, with the Apostle Paul, "The law of the Spirit of life in Christ Jesus hath made me free from the law of sin and death." Thus, in its full experience, sanctification is deliverance from the pollution, nature, and love of sin. To this we are every one called, that we may serve the Lord without fear, in holiness and righteousness before Him, all the days of our life....Yet the most holy Christian is still liable to temptation, is exposed to the subtle assaults of Satan, and can only continue to follow holiness as he humbly watches unto prayer, and is kept in constant dependence upon his Savior, walking in the light (1 John 1:7) in loving obedience of faith.[57]

The uniting conferences of 1892 and 1897 added certain "essential truths" to elaborate the Richmond Declaration, but the forces of liberalism were already in motion which would hold back this evangelical renewal among Friends for a half century—until post-World War II disillusion revealed the shallowness of modernist theology and provided opportunity both for doctrinal restatement and for leadership.

IN THE TWENTIETH CENTURY, then, the holiness message of the early Quakers split in two directions: *humanistic perfectionism* and *experiential perfectionism,* the first calling for social redemption based on the natural goodness of man, the second stressing the personal, emotional experience of heart purity, based on the premise that the natural man is utterly sinful—carnal. During the first decades of the twentieth century, the humanistic position seemed the strongest. Howard Brinton states of this modification of the Quaker prophetic ministry that it was more "Hellenistic than Hebraic...according to this view the highest in man is divine, and all Truth, whether reached by intuition or by a process of thought, is from God and truly inspired."[58]

Just as humanitarian service became the major outlet for more liberal Friends, so the holiness camp meeting and its missionary outreach became for the extreme holiness group an outlet for religious enthusiasm. Between these extremes moved the larger body of Friends, anxious to cherish the Quaker heritage, but confused about its present configurations. Some left the Society of Friends because of inroads of modernism. Others sought to hold the middle of the road—faithful in evangelism, faithful in service—while yet others became increasingly impatient with any sort of doctrine.

Rufus M. Jones wielded a tremendous influence during the first half of the century. A brilliant professor at Haverford College and world-renowned student of mystical religion, Jones voiced a moderate liberalism that carried the day for many American Quakers, and in the eyes of some, preserved it from ruinous obscurantism. Not one to blink at the reality of sin, Jones nevertheless taught a kind of humanistic holiness. Believing Christ to have possessed the "divine spark"—the "light within" as all people had, but in a perfect degree—no other course was possible but to consider that the human push to be Christlike constitutes humankind's holiness. As Christ overcame, so too men and women can open up to the life of God, for, he wrote, "The sundering gap between the divine and the human as formerly imagined does not exist."[59]

Unfortunately, Jones's teachings on perfection failed to stress Christ's atonement—the theological foundation for holiness. As is often the case with creative thinkers, his position was taken to extremes by some followers. His scholarly researches into Quakerism, his editorship of the *American Friend* for years, and his magnetic personal leadership made him by all odds the dominant voice in the first half of the twentieth century. With all due respect for the man, his position became vigorously, if politely, challenged, however, even by leaders within mainline Quakerdom. (Leaders from the independent evangelical yearly meetings never ceased to oppose the direction of his thought). For example, Lewis Benson, a Philadelphia Friend, in a penetrating little booklet, showed the disaster caused by "modern interpreters of Quakerism" stating that today's Quaker "has never actually been confronted with the original Quaker witness" but only the supposed "true essence" which is mysticism. He shows how the prophetic message had been lost through twisting the meaning of "inward light" into a connotation "of a native rational and ethical principle which is divine," in contradistinction to the early Quaker meaning (i.e., that "man is made spiritual and godly by a power which operates in man but which is...not of man.")[60]

Although the tug of humanism, with its Christ-denying teaching, gripped certain segments of Quakerdom, there were encouraging signs of evangelical renewal at mid-century. The theme of this book does not permit a complete evaluation of twentieth-century Quakerdom. But the following items indicate the direction of the swing away from the humanism advanced through the overoptimistic modernism of the 1920s and 1930s. Thomas R. Kelly's *Testament of Devotion* chronicled the thoughts of a Haverford professor's road back toward evangelicalism. Kelly wrote:

> But God inflames the soul with a burning craving for absolute purity. One burns for complete innocency and holiness of personal life....The blinding purity of God in Christ, how captivating, how alluring, how compelling it is.[61]

The books of popular theology by D. Elton Trueblood, professor of Religion, Earlham College, culminating in his deeper work, *A Philosophy of Religion,* spoke to the needs of war-torn peoples—Friend and non-Friend. His perceptive analysis of the sickness of Western civilization stemming from a disparity between ethical ideals and ethical practice have been influential. As a spokesman for liberals turning back toward more orthodox Christian faith, Trueblood emphasized these three vital points in the "new theology": realism about man's nature as a sinner, the uniqueness of the events of the Christian faith, and totality of the gospel in its relevance (yes, necessity) in this life and in the life eternal. Trueblood taught a progressive victory over sin. This is how he states it:

> Though the Bible urges us on to perfection it gives no encouragement to suppose that perfection is achieved. Of this we may be sure: a man who thinks he is righteous is not righteous. And he is not righteous for this reason, primarily, that he is full of spiritual pride, the most deadly form that sin can take.[62]

In his books Trueblood communicates in very readable prose the uniqueness of Jesus Christ. His analysis into the penetrating nature of sinful pride offered a healthy corrective to excesses of the holiness movement, especially its sometimes narrow, legalistic, view of sin. His teachings concerning the extent of the atonement and its provisions for holiness were less explicit than those proclaimed by earlier Quakers. Some wished to see in Trueblood a stronger emphasis upon the baptism with the Holy Spirit, with its purifying flames cleansing the hearts of believers.

Overshadowed by a more vocal modernism during early decades of the century, Quaker proponents of experiential holiness increasingly found fellowship with other evangelical churches in America that stressed a holiness message. So they attended and shared leadership in camp meetings with the "holiness churches"—Free Methodist, Pilgrim Holiness, Church of the Nazarene, and disenchanted Methodists—who made up the fellowship of the National Holiness Association. Antiliberal reaction tended to shift the holiness witness toward non-Quaker forms. Terminology—as well as interchurch fellowship—became mostly Wesleyan. Much missionary support during the 1920s and 1930s went to the National Holiness Missions (later known as World Gospel Mission). The Quaker peace witness was rejected, or given low priority, because it seemed to belong to the liberals, and because in those years social ethics had low priority in the ethos of the Wesleyan holiness movement.

Some prominent Quaker leaders transferred to other denominations. Others, however, held high the vision of a restored, evangelical Quakerism and labored patiently to that end. One of these people was Edward Mott, originally of New York Yearly Meeting. Under his leadership a Bible School had been established in Portland, Oregon. Elsewhere Western and Midwestern Quaker Bible schools were established to counteract colleges deemed too liberal in theology or too generalized in curriculum. These became training centers for a cadre of young ministers and leaders under whose direction and zeal the Church experienced growth and outreach. The latter part of the century witnessed an end to the Bible school era. An exception worth noting is Friends Bible College (now Barclay College) in Kansas, which has retained its identity as a Bible college. Some Bible schools became liberal arts colleges (e.g., Azusa Pacific in California and Malone in Ohio), and others yielded their existence to Quaker colleges reinvigorated by renewed constituent support and by leadership congenial to normative Quaker faith and practice (e.g., George Fox University in Oregon). These changes gave evidence that doctrines of holiness were no longer held in a separatist, revivalist mode but at the center of Quaker faith and practice.

T HE MID-TWENTIETH CENTURY witnessed signs of theological awakening among Friends. One movement, the Quaker Theological Discussion Group, arose in 1959 from the concern of several of young leaders eager for renewal of spiritual life among Friends. They represented various theological backgrounds. For half a century the group's journal, *Quaker Religious Thought*, has provided helpful forum for the exchange of theological insights, including those pertaining to the Quaker understanding of holiness.

A movement of larger general interest was the Association of Evangelical Friends. In some respects it resembled the movement that gave rise to the Richmond Conference of 1887. It attempted to bring unity and growth to Friends by a renewal of Christ-centered doctrines. At the first American Conference of Evangelical Friends, held in Colorado Springs, Colorado, in 1947, the aged Edward Mott pointed out in a final message—"The Transforming Power of Evangelical Faith"—the many scriptural references showing that people were called to be transformed from a carnal state to a new state—one of victory, in which a person "is enabled to live the new life in triumph."[63] Mott stressed the wholeness of the power of Christ.

This movement marked dissatisfaction both with the humanistic and experiential aspects of the Quaker doctrines of atonement, as exemplified by a narrow approach to Christian virtue through social service on the one hand, and through a narrow focus upon personal emotional experience on the other. It harked back to the early Quaker balance of experience and ethics in the Spirit-filled life. In the 1956 conference, held in Denver, Colorado, Friends predominantly from among the various Western and Midwestern yearly meetings reconfirmed the older doctrinal formulations (The Richmond Declaration of Faith, and Fox's Letter to the Governor of Barbados) and couched a brief statement in similar language. One of the stated purposes reads: "To promote among all Friends the sense of Christian responsibility for active participation in the speedy evangelization of the world, and to work for revival throughout Quakerdom, relying solely upon the moral power of truth and love and the dynamic of the Holy Spirit for the accomplishment of this task."[64]

Following a July 1959 conference held in Newberg, Oregon, a team led by Gerald Dillon, outgoing president of the association, embarked on a world tour of Friends missions, thus augmenting one of the concerns of the association—intervisitation among Friends in the interests of a Christ-centered spiritual awakening. During this same year, the *Concern,* dedicated to the evangelical message of Friends, began quarterly publication.

The Association of Evangelical Friends rose on the crest of vigorous Church extension and outreach among several American yearly meetings. Its leaders hoped for a renewal of spiritual life among *all* Friends, and envisioned a Friends Church evangelical in nature and worldwide in scope. In 1970 the Association disbanded, its leaders discerning that its task as a catalyst for renewal had been completed. The AEF spawned two significant offspring: a series of "Faith and Life" conferences involving many American yearly meetings, and the Evangelical Friends Alliance, which gathered hitherto independent evangelical yearly meetings into one organization. Through cooperative missionary outreach, Friends United Meeting, like a sister cluster of Friends groups, also developed; its worldwide membership now exceeds North American numbers.

The history of this catalytic movement is recorded in a book, *The Association of Evangelical Friends: A Story of Quaker Renewal in the Twentieth Century.*[65]

By the twenty-first century the cultural pressures upon the churches, including Friends, had muted the holiness testimony, especially in respect to personal spirituality. Analysis of this antinomian trend lies beyond the scope of this book. Suffice it to say that through writing and sermons a few years ago, under deep concern, I issued "A New Call to Holiness." More importantly, an excellent, definitive, study of holiness in the Quaker tradition was published in 2007. Entitled *Holiness: The Soul of Quakerism,* it is one in a series of studies in Christian history and theology published by Paternoster Press. The author, a professor at George Fox Evangelical Seminary, is Carole Dale Spencer.

The Friends Church—or Society of Friends, as some prefer to call it—now stands in a position to witness to the world a holiness message sufficiently deep to reach to sinful human nature, and sufficiently broad to reach out in the love of Christ in personal and social righteousness. In time of constant warring, as in the time of Fox, it is startling to the public to learn that there are people who claim to be sanctified and are also valiant for peacemaking. The combination is such that Quakers may by faithful witness yet serve to rally a fearful Church to the ways of her Savior and Lord.

THE CHURCH AS
COVENANT COMMUNITY

"The people, not the steeple
is the church"

The second major part of the theological legacy of Fox consists of his doctrine of the church. The Quaker movement sought to revive primitive Christianity, to rescue the church both from sacerdotalism and from secularism; and to restore it as a community of people separated from the world and drawn together by the Head, Jesus Christ. Seventeenth century England witnessed a revolution that had smoldered for a century (it had been ignited by a quarrel over vestments of the clergy) and had flamed out upon all phases of life—religious, political, and social—during that time. The Anglican aim, as propounded by Archbishop Laud prior to 1640, was that of religious unity signalized by common religious exercise, with the bishops—"true bearers of the sacraments"—ruling the church. Anglicanism was closely associated with the Stuart kings of England. Both Archbishop Laud and Charles I, however, were beheaded in the revolution that culminated in civil war and the Commonwealth period.

The Puritan brew, simmering under a lid of uniformity which Elizabeth had clamped on the religious pot, boiled over at mid-century. Puritanism called for a second reformation, one more spiritual than the one catering to Henry VIII's political, national, and marital interests. Puritanism emphasized both doctrine and experience; and the age bustled with pamphleteers proclaiming the journey of the saint on the way to heaven. A significant fruit of the movement was a renewed trust upon the Bible as the outward authority binding Christians together. The pope had long since been rejected by Puritans as the interpreter of Christian faith and practice, of course, and under the influence of Geneva the Marian exiles became increasingly Protestant and Calvinistic. With the removal of both king and archbishop, the principle of episcopacy in church polity was rejected.

Puritanism spoke with many voices quickened and made articulate by the reading of the Bible in a new translation King James had authorized in 1611. Puritan leaders sought to discover how authority and unity might develop based upon the outward authority of Scripture. To some the state (a "godly commonwealth") appeared to be the answer; to others the answer was a maintained religion, to ensure fidelity of the gospel. For this purpose a Committee of Triers was organized during Cromwell's leadership of England. Radical Puritans or "sectarians," as they are sometimes called, emphasized the "Inner Word," or Holy Spirit, as the interpreter of the written word. All Christians accepted, in theory at least, the authority of Scripture and the Lordship of Christ, but they differed as to how the "Word" of Scripture and the "Word" of personal religious experience could be reconciled. In short, they sought to rethink the doctrine of authority in the church. The radical Puritans, Quakers among them, agreed that no one church hierarchy or state could hand down religious certainty. This independent spirit that refused to accept any kind of *established* church arose from the Puritan insistence that spiritual truths can be individually experienced. Both liberty and unity were sought by these radical Puritans, but they seemed to be mutually exclusive. Eventually this dilemma came to be handled by a typically English compromise: Secularization of interests settled upon a principle of tolerance, where a principle of church authority had not. A nation that in the seventeenth century had fought with sword and word to hold together liberty and unity entered the eighteenth century with a secular tolerance substituting for the religious tolerance they could not find.

In the "Glorious Revolution" of 1688-1689, England brought back both king and established church but gave liberty and increasingly greater privilege to the dissenting groups of Christians. Just as the monarchy became constitutional and limited by the increasingly powerful parliament, so the Establishment became limited in its spiritual domain over the people. The Church of England retained prestige and favored status, certain economic advantages, but after that date it was no longer *the* church of the realm.

The issues of liberty and unity, quieted at the end of the eighteenth century, became issues again in the end of the turbulent twentieth century. The "Age of False Tolerance" as Arnold Toynbee calls it, had dissolved with the rediscovery that ideologies, not just boundaries and economic interests, stand at the core of conflict. Winthrop Hudson keenly observed that the Commonwealth period was

> one of the great creative periods in the history of the West. To the extent that the modern world has been the reflection of a dominant Anglo-Saxon culture, these two decades may almost be said to have produced the modern world.[66]

The decades that witnessed the birth and growth of the Quaker movement constituted a preview of struggles that occurred during subsequent centuries. Among Fox's contemporaries were forerunners of communists, church-state advocates, militant secularists, Separatists, and Christians who worked to sustain a free church in a free society. If one outstanding contribution is to be ascribed to Fox it is not his mysticism, his religious questing, his peace witness, nor his individualism, but his passionate and compelling conviction that the living Christ is gathering together his church as a holy community to witness his power within the world.

F OX DID NOT STAND ALONE in the seventeenth century in dreaming for such radical reformation of the church. Ideas of voluntary membership, separation of church and state, perfectionism, mysticism, the invisible church, expectation of the coming "new age"—such ideas appeared in various forms. At the outset of his ministry, bands of "Seekers" waited for the church, seeing no evidence of apostolic power until they heard the prophetic preaching of Fox, to which they responded gladly from 1652 on. The most radical group of the spiritual dispossessed were the Ranters. They despaired of an organized church and sought only the authority of individual expression, turning from corporate authority to the license of personal desire. They interpreted Christ's fulfilling of the law as a discharge of man's responsibility before the law. Hence it was no sin to do what before "conversion" was a sin. William Penn called this "a securer way of sinning than before: as if Christ came not to take away sin, but that we might sin more freely at his cost."[67]

The Ranters constituted the bitter dregs of Calvinism (although John Calvin would have shuddered at their immoral ways). They typify movements in every age that prostitute the grace of God and tend to drive the church back into the security of institutional control. Fox suffered six months imprisonment at Derby on charges of blasphemy, in accordance with an act aimed at the Ranters. Like the Dukhubors of Russia, these people had so lost their historical perspective concerning Christianity that they identified themselves with Christ. There is understandable warmth in the Quaker's words to one Ranter leader, "Repent, thou beast," and more than a handy metaphor in his castigation of them along with the Sodomites of the Old Testament. Such individualism challenged the very idea of a covenant community and stands in vivid contrast with Foxian emphasis upon the corporate witness of the church.

The Fifth Monarchy Men coupled an apocalypticism reflecting popular English sentiment that all institutions derived from William the Conqueror were corrupt—the "little horn" of Daniel's prophecy. The Norman conqueror's decisive victory over the English in 1066 is remembered by schoolboys. What these "Millerites" remembered, however, was the alliance William made with the pope. Their prophetic sign of the day of the Lord appeared to be the co-termination of monarchy derived from Rome, both on the Continent, in the blow given the Papacy by the Peace of Westphalia (1648), and within their own borders in the less subtle blow which severed Charles' head (1649). The group took up arms against London in 1661. Expecting the Lord's return a thousand years after the Council at Whitby (664, when the Celtic church rite was replaced by Roman ceremonies) they decided that King Jesus wanted from them tangible and supporting evidence of their faith before he returned. Such was the radical fringe associated with a rise in eschatological thinking. Many devout people longed for the personal return of Christ then as they do now. To this general expectancy Fox sounded the note that Christ—who will indeed come at the end of the age—is nevertheless present *now* to lead his people and that Christ's spiritual presence is real and vital among his gathered saints who must *now* fight his warfare—but with the Lord's own loving weapons!

The Levellers and the Diggers, represented by men such as Lilbourne and Winstanley, sought freedom of the spirit by equalizing material possessions. They were the socialists and communists of the day. The church they viewed as *only* invisible. For them the historic events of Christianity were treated as mythological symbols of struggles within society and within people (sounds modern, doesn't it?). For them the only visible and necessary corporate framework of society is the political state. They contributed, unwittingly perhaps, to a process of secularization that eventually discarded even the symbols of the Christian faith.

Among the Baptists, the "Finders," and the mystics are found ideas antecedent and corresponding to those Fox stressed. Early on Fox addressed audiences that included the General Baptists, who taught voluntary membership, insisted upon a knowledgeable confession of faith, and supported the separation of church and state. Puritanism contained a strain of mysticism, carried over through Anabaptist, Schwenckfeld, and Boehmist influences in part, but fused with Bible-centered evangelicalism. It was concerned with the church as well as with the individual soul. Mysticism served as a powerful leaven to produce a hunger for authentic, individual, spiritual certainty in people dissatisfied by existing authorities.

An appraisal of these turbulent times by a social historian, Ernst Troeltsch, is trenchant:

> All that remained of the mystical upheaval was "the Children of the Light" or the "Society of Friends"....In the final form of their doctrine they are the direct descendants of the spirituality of the Reformation period....In reality the Society of Friends represents the union of this mystical doctrine [the presence of the Divine Light of Christ] with

the Baptist ideal of the pure and holy voluntary community based on genuine conversion and freedom from State control.[68]

Fox's contribution as a spiritual reformer needs to be seen against this background of the seventeenth-century search for the church. There is a touch of humor, but also a sort of judgment upon those who ignore Fox the churchman, in his summary of a dispute at Leicester: "But I maintained the true church, and the true head thereof, over the heads of them all, till they all gave out and fled away."[69]

The false church that "fled away" before Fox certainly constituted a large proportion of those who called themselves Christian! His indictment fell on all "sects" and "opinions" that are overturned by the judgments of Christ. An analysis of Fox's writings shows that he considered the church apostate along four basic lines: *impure conduct, empty forms, unworthy methods of maintenance, and inadequate doctrines.*

"Where is your service of God," he queried professional religionists and parish-holders "so long as your hearts run after lusts and pleasures...as bowling, drinking, hunting, hawking, and the like. If these have your heads, God will not have your lips."[70]

As a sober Puritan he heaped wrath upon giddy, gaudy Cavalier frivolity. "How doth the devil garnish himself," he exclaimed in a prelude to an indictment upon powdered hair and a "store of ribands [ribbons]." In his indictment of extravagant display, he reminds one of a stormy second-century Christian leader, Tertullian. Fox denounced the sin of greed in various ways. He called magistrates to repent, lawyers to stop oppression, farmers and merchants to consider other values than gain. Both the poor and the rich are guilty of greed. "This is the word of the Lord to you," he wrote to merchants. "Ask no more than you will have for your commodity, and keep to yea and nay...and so you will come to show a life like Christians...so a child shall trade with you as a man."[71]

Greed has sucked the morality out of religion and made the profession of Christianity meaningless. It must be answered by non-attachment to possessions. Cruelty in that era was marked by frequent and arbitrary hangings; and Fox himself was set upon with stones, sticks, and even struck on the head by a heavy, bound Bible, all by professing Christians who objected to his preaching. Fox censured the church's substitution of form for content. If morality was low it was because religion had not met man at the place of his ethical needs. In a negative way, Puritanism had reacted to this situation: Parliament soldiers in Oxford fired shots at the statue of the Blessed Virgin and Child, for example, and in other destructive ways reacted against Roman formalism. Although Fox shared these feelings, he rejected violent protest. His doctrine, as the historian Gardiner puts it, "was but the quintessence of Puritan protest against external formality." Included in the Quaker's catalog of the "dark inventions of fallen man" were altars, crucifixes, images, pictures, organs, pipes, whistles, singing boys, singing of prayers, praying by beads, formal prayers, formal singing, formal preaching, processioning, gowning of priests with white sleeves, surplices, tippets, hoods, caps, red gowns, mitres, the cardinal's cap, and the pope's triple crown! Add, also, feast days and pagan names for the days of the week.

F OX PROTESTED FORMALISM more thoroughly than most Commonwealth religious parties. The semi-established "Independency" of Cromwell he considered hypocritical; and in addition to the expected criticism against "priestcraft," he

objected to using the term *church* for that which was made
of lime, stones, and wood. The antipathy for steeplehouses
(as he called them) stemmed from his belief that they were
barriers instead of means to bring people to God. People
prayed the Lord's Prayer but did not know the Lord or
forgive others as they prayed. In company with other
extreme Puritans, Fox considered that the "two sacraments"
bound the church to a dead, formal religion. Hence in the
search for the immediacy of Christian experience, he believed
that sprinkling infants and using communion wine and bread
were of "the letter" and not the true means of grace. To a
"papist" (Roman Catholic) Fox pointed out that there is no
Scripture for "throwing a little water in a child's face" and
calling it "baptized." Whereas infant sprinkling was regarded
as a "dark invention," believer's baptism—so stressed by the
Anabaptists on the Continent—he viewed as an unnecessary
and uninspired return to an earlier, Old Testament
dispensation. The breaking of bread, likewise, need not
continue in a ceremony with material objects. "The bread
which the saints break is of the body of Christ; he is the
bread of life."[72]

The early Quakers "pamphleteered" vigorously against
the Church of England for unworthy methods of maintenance. The charge indicted a state-supported and "un-called"
clergy. In a colorful polemic entitled "The Mystery of the
Great Whore Unfolded," Fox declared that all sects had been
made drunk "with the wine of fornication." With these apoca-
lyptic words he revealed the apostate condition of a church
that forcefully maintained itself through a professional,
nonspiritual ministry.

Fox wanted reform "head and tail," and not just "root
and branch," as the anti-episcopal petition of 1640 had called
for. Even Cromwell hedged on reform: He tried to reestablish

state religion and refused to abolish compulsory tithes to support it. In an intensely scathing passage Fox shows the continuing degeneracy of the "hireling ministry," as the "common-prayer men" (Anglican) forced out the papists, then the Presbyterians forced out the "common-prayer men," and finally the Independents engaged in the same campaign of forceful monopoly. All the while the "popish dregs" of persecution and merchandised religion remained to poison the church.[73]

It should be remembered that the Quakers suffered much loss of goods and people for their refusal to conform to compulsory state tithes for church support. Their steadfastness in this witness left a legacy of church-state separation, in company with that left by the other dissenters in Baptists and Congregational movements. In America today we sometimes take this free church tradition for granted and forget at what cost it came.

If compulsory tithes for state support of the ministry was bad, even worse was the bypassing of the gifts of God by "hireling ministers." At this juncture Fox was not against ministers as such. He was against ministers who had no divine calling. The disillusion of the one who, as a youth gained an insight that education at Cambridge or Oxford didn't qualify folks to be ministers, ripened into conviction that unspiritual clergy were "Simon Magus brats" and "of the spirit of Gehazi," who bought their gifts at schools and colleges, sold them again for money, and took payment for the grace of God. Such false prophets make merchandise of the people; they are "hirelings who fleece the sheep for their own gain."[74]

Fox averred that persecution is the means whereby false religion tries to perpetuate itself. Those who "will not have

Christ to reign over them" turn to the sword to support their institutions. This indictment included the New England Puritans!

Impure conduct, empty forms, and unworthy methods of maintenance evidence the apostatized church, but the source of evil must be considered doctrinal. Specifically, the church was charged with having lost the power of Christ amid accretions of tradition and ceremony. Roman Catholicism had lost the "real presence of Christ" in the mass, Protestantism in the letter of Scriptures, Ranterism in libertinism, Fifth-Monarchists in apocalypticism, and the Leveller movement in politics. Accordingly, the real power of Christ in atonement was not experienced. In these ways the atonement became artificial and forensic. Fox wrote:

> The Papists say they must have a purgatory when they are dead. And the Protestants say they must have a body of death and sins of the flesh, whilst on this side the grave, and that there is no perfection while upon the earth.[75]

There is no need to talk about the blood of Christ, believed Fox, unless it really cleanses the heart from sin.

Positively, then, George Fox considered the Church of the Restoration as the company of those gathered out of the world by the grace of God, through Jesus Christ. Richard Baxter, Puritan divine, scoffed at the Quaker claim. It might be expected, he reasoned, for them to reproach the church, "but to appropriate it to themselves that are no members of it" smacked of insolence.[76]

The Quakers, however, affirmed the true church in a high, but nonliturgical, nonpriestly sense, like the Anabaptists on the Continent with their emphasis upon the Church of the Restitution, who gathered in the name of Christ and without state support. The church, they believed, is *gathered out of the world* through the revelation of God, in the power of Jesus Christ, who effects the restoration of humankind in holiness. The church *in the world* is as a gospel fellowship, a gospel order, a holy community, and a fellowship of evangelism.

CONCERNING REVELATION; early Friends said it was not enough to acknowledge the Bible to be inspired. One must, also, know the Inspirer if one is to understand Scripture aright; otherwise the meaning of Scripture becomes judged by tradition, by papal authority, or by unguided reason. One who knows Jesus Christ experimentally knows the revelation of God about which the Scriptures speak authentically. Scriptures are the *words of God,* Jesus Christ is the *Word of God.* Unless the Holy Spirit guides, Scriptures become just what natural man says they are. Fox frequently stated that "none can understand their writings aright without the same Spirit by which they were written"[77]; he was willing to trust the inspiration of the Bible to the same Inspirer who transmits the truths. Anglicanism trusted that reason could appropriate the interpretations transmitted by "the Holy Fathers and Doctors of the Church, as they had received it from those before them." John Calvin affirmed but hesitated to proclaim "that he only whom the Holy Spirit hath persuaded, can repose himself on the scripture with a true certainty."[78] Even the Westminster Confession (Presbyterian) asserted that the "inward work of the Holy Spirit" gives full persuasion and assurance of infallibility.[79]

Fox added to these general evangelical affirmations a bold affirmation of the *actual* present revelation whereby the Holy Spirit leads individual Christians and the church in unity with scriptural revelation. The Holy Spirit cannot be institutionalized within hierarchy nor bound by tradition. The true church understands the will of God directly by the leadership of Jesus Christ, who speaks through written Scriptures and by direct illumination of the Holy Spirit.

The Quaker attitude toward Scripture was misunderstood by Roger Williams, contemporary Baptist, and has been misunderstood by other evangelicals since that time. Regrettably, too, some Friends over the years failed to appreciate that early teaching. A position that aimed at enhancing the work of Christ as head of his church became twisted into a position that enhanced human judgment and minimized the authority of revealed Scripture. This disregard for the centrality of the present Christ, and resulting ignorance of the Bible, impoverished the Quaker movement in the eighteenth and nineteenth centuries. Although clearly affirming the Bible as a unique and final record of the salvation offered in Christ, Quakers stressed that the church must and can be inspired and led by Christ.

For Fox and early Friends, the Scriptures were the standard for doctrine. They sought to couch their arguments in its terms, rather than in scholastic phrasing, in order to more closely maintain integrity in doctrinal formulations. Rachel King correctly stated that Fox did not claim beliefs, doctrines, or principles that he did not think are recorded in the Bible, and certainly "never [claimed] that the direct inspiration has revealed anything to him that supersedes New Testament teaching."[80]

In 1655, Fox wrote thus to Oliver Cromwell:

> For now the state of this present age is, that the Lord is bringing his people into the life the Scriptures were given forth from, in which life people shall come to have unity with God, with Scriptures and one another, for the establishing of righteousness, truth, and peace, in which is the kingdom of God.[81]

The Scriptures provide our outward rule of conduct. They reveal what has happened redemptively up through the coming of Christ. Present revelation confirms and applies this past revelation. What the more staid religionists of the seventeenth and eighteenth centuries called "enthusiasm" was charged against the Quakers. Henry More revealed the Anglican horror for such teachings when he defined *enthusiasm* as "nothing else but the misconceit of being inspired," and avers that "if ever Christianity be exterminated, it will be by Enthusiasm."[82]

FOR FOX THE REVERSE WAS TRUE: If ever Christianity be *established* and the church restored it will be by the inspiration of the Holy Spirit. What gave him confidence in present inspiration? Not a humanistic assertion of the divinity of man, but rather a bold appropriation of basic evangelical teaching regarding the reality of the risen Lord. The church gathered through revelation finds its implementation through Christ, often referred to as the "Light Within," but *never* by the term *inner light*. The concept of "inner light," when drawn away from its context and under the impact of deism, modernism, or naturalism, has come to mean almost anything generally and nothing particularly. In considering Fox's view of Jesus Christ, it must be remembered that Puritans emphasized the spiritual birth, not the nativity, and the pilgrimage of Christians through life to heaven, not from Jerusalem to Golgotha. Not a denial of the historical foundations, it was rather a revolt from a ritualizing of the heritage by the Roman Catholics. Fox discerned rightly that secularism "couched at the door" of this reaction. Spiritual pilgrimage can degenerate into materialistic treks. This was evidenced by the Levellers and, especially, by the Diggers, for whom the Christian story became just symbolic of economic struggle. One leader, Winstanley, believed the church remained always invisible, the commonwealth alone is visible, and all kingdom work must issue through government that must with equity dole out the good earth "wherein a man receives his nourishment and preservation."[83]

It remained for Karl Marx two centuries later to formulate a more precise materialism out of the human pilgrimage, with Christian symbols ripped off. Because of the tremendous impact of this system of economics upon the twentieth century, Fox certainly understood the dangers implicit in such radical Puritan movements. His Protestant detractors unfairly called him "papistic" because he affirmed Christ's direct guidance of the covenant community. The objectors failed to understand the Quaker's hope for a balance between the historic and the experiential, the objective and the subjective. Through the teaching about Christ the Light this balance is asserted and the nature of the church delineated. This prophetic insight about the nature of the church offers direction for church renewal in our times.

Lewis Benson has stated aptly that "Fox's doctrine of the Church can only be understood in the light of his doctrine of Christ."[84] Fox wrote: "Now all that you call Christendom do believe that Christ is come, and is risen, and that Jesus is Christ the Son of God; so that now they are all to receive him, and to walk in him, and abide in him." There are two proofs given by the apostles, he continued, "to prove that Jesus was the Christ by Moses and the law, and the prophets," and "to prove and examine themselves, whether or not Jesus Christ was within them."[85]

Although much of the Quaker preaching proclaimed the immediacy of spiritual experience of Christ, it should never be forgotten that it is the once-offered Jesus Christ who "speaks to the condition" of searching, sinful people. It's the real Pascal Lamb, whose blood wet the hillside in Palestine, who speaks to the human condition. This theme appears constantly throughout Fox's "doctrinals." (It is a sad commentary upon the theological poverty of present-day Friends and students of religion that whereas the *Journal* has been oft-printed and much read as a classic of spiritual introspection, Fox's doctrinal writings have been ignored and only infrequently read.) Throughout his writings appear frequent references to the blood of Christ. This paragraph portrays his teaching about atonement in Christ:

> And we that do believe in the light of Christ, which is the life in him, cannot deny the flesh of Christ, our heavenly bread, who remains in the heavens. I say that Jesus Christ that died without the gates of Jerusalem above sixteen hundred years since, who hath enlightened us with his heavenly divine light...through which light we are grafted into Christ...who hath saved, redeemed, and purchased and bought us with his precious blood, the blood of the heavenly man, the second Adam, who does cleanse and sanctify us with his blood, the blood of the new covenant, Christ Jesus; so I say...we are...to live unto him and be ordered, ruled, and governed by him.[86]

Thus the union of Jesus of Nazareth and Golgotha with Christ the Light is clearly stated. The church must not be denied her Lord by the obstructing forms of ritual, letter, or symbol. The church must be emancipated from the shadows of the Old Covenant. God speaks now in the tabernacle of the soul. Certitude arises not by detachment from God for a "better look" but by receiving God's revelation into the consciousness of experience. Various terms are used by Fox to describe the activity of God within the soul. The *measure within, the Holy Ghost, the spirit of truth, the cross within, the life, the anointing, the substance,* and *the second Adam.*

The term *Christ* is used many times unmodified. Four main categories into which the terms fall may be noted: *Christ the Word, Christ the Light, Christ the Seed,* and *Christ the Life.* The first—Christ the Word—denotes the authority of God in revealing himself personally to the world, the *logos* of continuing revelation. The second depicts the way by which Christ exposes evil in man and brings him into unity with God—a description in one term of the functions of law and grace. In this connection it should be observed that the term *spark,* or *divine spark* has absolutely no relevance to early Quaker thought! Despite its use by some modern Friends, it is *not* a synonym for *Light Within.* Others share my view on this. For example, both Rachel King and Howard Brinton have noted that the usage falsely implies complete immanence and division of spiritual illumination.[87]

The Light was never divorced from its Christological relationship by founders of the Quaker movement. That is, Jesus Christ and George Fox were not both illumined by a common entity. Fox wrote a little paper "to show how the Lord was come to teach his people himself by his own son Christ Jesus," in which this point is made clear.[88] It remained for Robert Barclay in his *Apology for the True Christian Divinity* to give detailed emphasis upon what he terms "the Universal and Saving Light."

The reference to Christ the Seed has reference to redemptive history in accordance with the Genesis accounting of the "seed of the woman" bruising the serpent's head. The promise to Abraham, thought Fox, referred not to many but to *one seed,* which is Christ; which seed "bruises the head of the serpent."[89] The term refers to election in Christ.

Christ the Life is descriptive of the moral and spiritual authentication of God in man's life. This is the state into which the restored ones are brought from the bondage of sin and death. Thus it is seen that Fox holds a unitary view of the historic and inward Christ that extends the Puritan emphasis upon Christ in experience and also strengthens the historic moorings of that experiential faith.

The church that comes by revelation of God and in the power of Jesus Christ calls people out of the world by restoring their spiritual natures. The perfectionist (holiness) doctrine of salvation has already been delineated. Suffice it here to correlate this to Fox's doctrine of the church. God is restoring a people unto himself. The risen Lord is actively within his world drawing those who believe into unity. Fox's interpretation is a protest against the tendency of Calvinism to identify a certain group as the special, spiritual Israel. Indeed, for the Quakers, Christ is the elected one, the chosen seed! All who come to him are chosen of God. They become complete, become transformed in Christ. His doctrine of the election in the seed is an extension of the *scope* of salvation, as his doctrine of perfection is an extension of the *intensity* of salvation in moral terms.

For early Friends, the church in the world is a gospel fellowship, a gospel order, a holy community, and a fellowship of evangelism. George Fox had confidence that it was God's purpose to restore the unity of people through "the true church faith." Unity with God, with the Scriptures, and with one another is his cry. In a general letter sent out in 1662, Fox wrote of the Quakers that

> they come to the church that is in God, and the fellowship which is the *gospel* fellowship, which is the power of God, in which is stability....In this is the church fellowship with Christ in God, which will stand; for the gospel is everlasting; the church of God is the *pillar and ground of truth.*[90]

Fox's frequent references to the "church" is somewhat startling to a casual observer accustomed to the later usage (since 1800) of the "Society of Friends," and who has concluded that Quakers made no claim to be the church. The real presence of Christ makes possible the real fellowship of those who together know the mystery of the new birth and the leadership of the Christ. Such people do not need outward crosses of wood or stone to remind them, for they "feel Christ and his cross." Nor do they need to idolize "temples" and steeplehouses, for the church "is the *people* which Christ is the head of."[91]

This legacy has been somewhat dissipated among Friends in recent times. Whereas some Friends may not use the term *church* for the building—preferring *meetinghouse*—sadly, neither do they use the term *church* for the people! Using subordinate terms, such as *Friends*, *Friends of Truth*, or the eventual *Society of Friends* wasn't meant to discredit the idea of the church but to enhance its more inclusive meaning, of which particular fellowship is one part.

This fellowship of Christians is external. The gospel fellowship not only contains the spiritually reborn, it finds them in deliberate and active participation. On the one hand Fox sought to avoid institutionalism; on the other, he sought to avoid a subjectivism which rendered the church "invisible."

The church is the "elect seed of God," with a covenantal relationship; thus "apostolicity"—one of the marks of the church—is continuous among the particular people who are called in Christ. The "catholicity" of the church is to be found in the universality of its Christ. Hence those who recognize his voice, see his light, and follow after him become the body of Christ. The holy fellowship is also a visible gospel fellowship in which the Lord Christ Jesus comes "to teach his people himself."

The term *gospel order* denoted Quaker Church polity, an attempt to establish meetings for worship according to what Fox believed was the apostolic pattern. Part of this order included what might be called the "contemporary apostolate." God who commissioned the Twelve and Paul of Tarsus still commissions people to serve his church. The transmission of the gospel is not through ecclesiastical laying on of hands to preserve an unbroken line of bishops, but rather by the commissioning of the Holy Spirit. The key to the Quaker organization lies in the term which bespeaks this divine commissioning—*recognition*. The gifts of God require implementation, and the spiritual discernment of true Christians suffices to *recognize* these gifts and thus to give opportunity for their exercise. "All that were heirs of the power of God," wrote Fox, "were to take their possession of the power of God, the gospel and its order."[92] This included evangelism, ministry, worship, relief of sufferings, settling of differences, discipline of offenders, and the regulation of social life in the community of Christ.

The form by which this "gospel order" became established among Friends consisted of a system of "meetings." Prior to 1666, by which time persecution and schism had made havoc with the churches, a system of "particular" or local meetings, and "general" or area gatherings, obtained, in which traveling ministers by their presence or writings aided local overseers. Between 1667 and 1680 the grouping of particular meetings into "monthly meetings" and of representative "quarterly" and "yearly" meetings took place. The ministers had a general meeting in connection with the yearly meeting at London. In addition, ministers in and around London met each Sunday morning (before dispersing for

117

services) and also on Monday, forming what was called the "second day's morning meeting," which had oversight over the spoken and written ministry of Friends. By his wish this group picked up the mantle of leadership upon Fox's death.[93] The "Meeting for Suffering" grew beyond the legal and physical care of the oppressed: The weekly representative gathering became an executive body.

This is the pattern of church organization that has persisted in general outline throughout the centuries. The polity originally was rather resilient, somewhat *"de facto"* in that those with concerns took leadership. Unity resulted, not through arbitrary vote or appeal to precedent, but through the representation of manageable corporate units, sensitive to the leadership of the Holy Spirit. The yearly meeting, or annual gathering of those so constituted geographically as to have adequate interaction, remains the highest authority of the Church, regardless of the various inter-yearly meeting fellowships or enterprises to which support may be delegated. Normative Quaker polity is neither episcopal nor congregational, but representational.

Throughout the early chapters of the Quaker story are paragraphs of tension resulting from the contest of individualism versus corporate unity. William Mucklow, in the "hat-controversy" attacked the "Foxonian-unity," which he claimed was based on the assumption that "the Power of God in Friends" resided only within the ruling group of London ministers. But regardless of some failures in practice, the theory was rightly adhered to that the Holy Spirit can lead the individual and the group together in a powerful way. The biblical pattern is depicted in Acts and defined by Paul in 1 Corinthians 12. "Every member in the church hath an office: and...is serviceable," stated Fox, indicating that not only should the Church recognize and separate for their ministry the gifted ministers, but that the Church ought to recognize God's gifts at every level. Quakers not always have been able to nurture individual gifts, as the theory calls for—sometimes the machinery has stifled initiative through its obsolescence—yet over the years the Quakers have demonstrated to a marked degree this blending of individual concern and corporate blessing.

Early Friends held three kinds of meetings, public meetings for evangelizing the unconverted (sometimes called "threshing meetings"); meetings for worship, unpopular in those days and attended almost entirely by convinced Friends; and meetings for the transaction of business.[94] All were to be equally under the leadership of the Spirit. Theoretically, no difference should exist between meetings for worship and for business. In waiting upon the Lord, and feeling his power, they are to be led of him. Christ is in the midst, whatever the nature of the meeting. This is a rich part of the Quaker legacy. True worship must always be in the *silence of the flesh,* that is, under the dominion of the Spirit, so that the preaching, praying, and singing truly give inspired service. The worship meetings were of two sorts: One, the "retired" meeting, was given over mainly to quiet waiting; the other, more frequent in early years, was devoted mainly to preaching or exhortation, although based on devotional silence.

Over the years Friends have sought to hold to traditional ways and yet to adapt to contemporary needs. They have not always been successful. The emergence of the pastoral system in the nineteenth century marked a vigorous attempt to recoup the membership losses quietism had produced. Meetings in America, patterned somewhat after Methodist or Baptist services, provided, nonetheless, an opportunity for public evangelism in the spirit of the earlier "threshing meetings," as well as for the biblical instruction of converts and the children of Friends. If pastoral Friends are sometimes uninstructed in the use of exhortation and prayer in open meetings, their departure from an earlier pattern may not be so serious as the departure of "quiet meetings" from the burden of aggressive evangelism.

Early Friends sought to restore a prophetic ministry both to worship and to evangelism. An exhortation concludes:

> And therefore all Friends, that are come to witness the Holy Ghost and faith, in which the true praying and building is, which gives victory over the world, as you are moved, speak; for they spake as they were moved by the Holy Ghost, as the spirit gave them utterance.[95]

No mass or common prayer book is needed by those who have the Spirit who gave forth the Scriptures! Hearts awakened by the Holy Spirit understand those who wrote in the power of the Holy Spirit. The Lord's Supper is claimed by Fox on the basis of its fulfillment in Christ. He makes a distinction between the supper which Jesus shared with his disciples the last night before he was betrayed and the supper of the risen and ascended Lord. The first was "to show forth the Lord's death until he come."[96] It pointed the way beyond the death and resurrection when Christ would drink the fruit of the vine anew in the kingdom of God, words fulfilled as Jesus ate with the disciples and was known in the breaking of the bread. After the ascension, "the churches were gathered" but "as yet they were not come off many outward elementary things."[97] Accordingly, Christ sent John to call the church to another supper: "Behold, I stand at the door and knock: if any man hear my voice, and open the door, I will come in to him, and will sup with him, and he with me....he that hath an ear, let him hear what the spirit saith unto the churches" (Revelation 3:20-22 KJV).[98]

Fox would not limit the supper to a testimonial of the past presence of Christ nor clothe him within exclusive elements of the bread and wine. He called for a real, spiritual participation in the life of the ascended Lord, consonant with Jesus words, "Unless you eat the flesh of the Son of Man and drink his blood, you have no life in you" (John 6:53).

S OCIALLY, the church is the holy community, drawn together out of apostasy and darkness into true union with God. For this reason marriage within the holy community ought to be treated under the care of the church and not secularized, under the care of the state, as popular Puritanism had done. Here again is a "high-church," nonliturgical view. The Roman Church conceived of marriage as a sacrament to be directed by the priestly offices; reactionary Protestant Puritanism, partly under the "new Israel" idealism, thought of marriage as within the province of the godly commonwealth. In the year 1653, Fox advocated a plan for marriage by which the couple should lay the matter "before the faithful," secure the clearance of church and relatives, and take one another in an appointed meeting witnessed by not fewer than twelve people. This was the same year that the Barebones Parliament had passed an act making compulsory a civil ceremony before a justice of the peace. People who had been spiritually restored by Christ ought to be joined by him and in his will, believed the Quakers. Believers were forbidden to marry unbelievers and thus to depart from the spirit by which they had been brought into God's family. Quakers aimed to recapture marriage as an institution of God, restoring the sacramental ideal, basing its sanctity on experiential faith. They enhanced marriage as a relationship standing at the very center of the Christian society. In the approval of the congregation, the spiritual joining of a man and a woman in marriage is witnessed. This is another example of the early Quaker attempt at balancing individual and corporate "leadings." That the church should thus enter "normal" affairs of life attested to the "wholeness" that characterized the Quaker approach. In the light of the contemporary quest for holistic faith, the early Quaker pioneers were prophetic.

The holy community of the church included a covenant-like concern for the instruction of children both in some "lawful calling" and also in the truths of the gospel, remembering that it is the Lord "that brings to the birth, and gives power to bring forth, whether it be natural or spiritual...and the souls of all are in his hand and power."[99]

It is a sad commentary on the second-generation Friends that they ran on the momentum of early trained leaders. In measure Quakers did recover the vision of education—many schools have been established by Friends over the years—but education and evangelism did not keep hand in hand. In consequence Friends at times became educational benefactors for others at the expense of their own evangelistic outreach.

The holy community of the Church included whoever looked for guidance from Christian people. The masters of families in Barbados were encouraged to include "negroes and tawny Indians" in their instructions, or to entrust them to others for the task. The meetings looked out for the widows and the fatherless, for apprenticing "poor Friends' children." They provided hospitals for the aged and asylum for "distempered people." Thus did the Church become a holy community colonizing within the world, sometimes withdrawn and defensive and dwindling, but at other times vibrantly on the offense, evangelistic, and increasing in numbers. Presently increase in numbers occurs most significantly in the so-called "'Global South"—in Latin America, Africa, and Asia.

Out of an extended concern for her own people, in looking after their mundane affairs amid afflictions of an often hostile world, came a practice that almost proved to be harmful to Quakers—birthright membership. In the middle of the eighteenth century, for purposes of clarification, those were considered member families who subscribed to Poor Relief.[100] Separated from the closely defining bounds of persecution and withdrawn from active evangelism, the movement of the Quakers was hampered by a perversion of one of its strongest features—the bond of community. Like the colonial "half-way covenant," birthright membership so broadened the base of community as to destroy spiritual fellowship. The new ethnic circle, increasingly strengthened by custom, inter-family marriage, special testimonies, and business ties, nearly strangled the Friends movement until steps were taken in most yearly meetings to abolish it, or at least to circumvent such membership as an index of vitality. Birthright membership nevertheless still remains a convenient crutch, in the older Quaker centers, for all too many spiritually uncommitted people who prize their genealogy but not their heritage.

Contemporary Friends are rethinking membership, forced by the times to draw sharper ideological lines. One trend is toward a humanistic definition that omits the necessity of spiritual rebirth, or even overt Christian language, but the other—gratifyingly—is toward a renewal of emphasis upon definite spiritual conversion and commitment to Quaker beliefs.

Early Friends comprised a company of private and public evangelists. They felt that the Lord was ushering in a revival of the apostolic church after the "long dark night of apostasy." Claiming the same power of the Holy Spirit that moved the early church, the Quaker movement easily took root in the English soil prepared by the dormant years of ultra-Calvinism and the plowing of Independent and Baptist lay preaching. The "order" of the ministry was extended to those who heard God's command to go and teach all nations. Early Friends believed fervently that God had made such called ones "to be his mouth."[101] These ministers were to "spread themselves abroad," to "trample upon all deceit," to answer the witness of God in men. Not all Friends were to do public evangelization. According to an ancient epistle, Fox admonished that some should wait in their own meeting place while "three, or four, or six, that are grown up strong...go...and thresh the heathenish nature."[102]

THE STRENGTH of the early movement lay in these "public Friends" who could witness undaunted before high (emperor of Austria) and low as ministers "valiant for the truth upon the earth." In what seems to this sophisticated age unwarranted effrontery, Fox wrote to various kings and rulers admonishing them to turn to Christ. He was confident Christ's true ministers could turn the world upside down without crying for magistrates to help them out with "staff, and sword, and bag, and gaols."

From this sober vantage point the affair seems utopian until one considers that Protestants had not given themselves seriously to missions at this time, being preoccupied with political affairs, national reforms, and doctrines of divine election that muffled interest for the great commission. Early Friends stood in the company of the Waldensees, the Moravians, and certain pietistic Lutherans who grasped the essential call to worldwide evangelization. Confident that Christ, the Light, shines upon the conscience of all people, to blind in judgment or to lead to truth, the Quakers wanted to answer that witness of God in everyone. (The phrase "that of God in every man" has been misunderstood by some moderns who accept a "little-spark-of-God-in-every-man theory." Fox meant by this expression simply what John teaches about the unity of the eternal "Word" and Jesus of Nazareth and his witness to everyone for condemnation or assurance.) Their ministry was to lead people past profession into possession of the very life of Christ, to teach the gospel and thus to become channels whereby Christ would lead people out of their sins into the family of God.

Friends looked upon the ministry as a distinct calling both for the evangelizing of the world and the edification of worshipers. All people may be "confessors" of Christ, "though they are not ministers and apostles."[103] The calling of God, whether for a limited itinerary or for longer ministry, is the essential preparation. Voluntary support of a true minister was stated to be an acceptable and scripturally-warranted practice. In 1653, Fox wrote that "if any minister of Jesus Christ...which Jesus Christ sends forth...comes to our houses, and ministers unto us spiritual things, we will set before him our carnal things; and he that soweth unto us spiritual things, it is the least that we minister unto him of our carnal things."[104]

It was *compulsory* support of state-appointed, uncalled ministers against which Fox fulminated. To those who feared ministry would cease if maintenance were taken away, Fox answered that such a ministry *ought* to collapse; but that the power of a true ministry would "open the hearts of people...and make them give to you that there would be no want."[105]

Fox's advice for the gospel order included this:

> That care be taken from time to time, as Friends are moved thereunto, for relieving faithful Friends' necessities, and for other services of truth...that ministering Friends may not be cumbered with outward things, but kept out of them.[106]

This quaint but powerfully stated principle of a released ministry has not been fully appreciated. It is abundantly clear that early Friends took care of the needs of itinerating Friends for shorter or longer periods of ministry. Although Fox gave high premium to release of preachers, since the rise of the pastoral ministry some nonpastoral Friends, in an effort to avoid what they considered was a major defection toward a "hireling ministry," have more readily provided release for many other ministries—reconstruction, office work for meetings, teaching—than for preaching, pastoral or otherwise. These Friends have sought to guard the meetings for worship from the dominance of a professionally trained, paid minister, lest his leadership suppress free participation by other Friends. But if, as it must be admitted, the voices of public exhortation by the many have been muted by the pastoral minister within the yearly meetings utilizing this system, to a *larger degree* the prophetic voice of the recognized minister has been lost to Friends and to the world. If Friends can accept a pastoral ministry—Spirit-filled, Spirit-called, and recognized and released for the work—and at the same time maintain a variety of meetings so the gifts of all may be exercised, then the heart of the Quaker gospel order will be rediscovered. The call of God for the ministry, the recognition of the gift by the Church, and voluntary support are the necessary ingredients. Beyond that the nature of the needs ought to govern. Perhaps if Friends could look about them with greater objectivity they would cease to strain out the gnats: for the whole pattern of state-supported ministry has broken down, and professionalism is abhorred by evangelical denominations who stress the truly spiritual vocation of the minister. The minister among Friends is not a "man of the cloth," but a man or a woman specially gifted of God. In clamoring for the exercise of gifts Friends sometimes have forgotten that if God bestows gifts involving leadership, that leadership ought to be accepted by his church. Early Friends sought to walk the narrow path between "no ministry" and "hireling ministry." It is a worthy path, trod with difficulty. Because of present-day urban diversification of economy, Ellwood's answer to the early-day criticism of Rogers is strikingly relevant:

> May none beyond Seas go but who can spare
> Sufficient of their own the charge to bear?
> Must Christ be so confin'd he may not send
> Any but such as have Estates to spend?
> God bless us from such Doctrine and such Teachers
> As will admit of none but wealthy Preachers.[107]

The gift of the ministry was regulated among Friends. God ordains, the Church records that ordination. Certificates of approval were early given in order to avoid cranks and crackpots. Here again is that balance between individual and corporate judgment, a balance that has meaning only if the real presence and direction of the Teacher is understood. Otherwise it becomes a mockery of the gospel by devices of prestige-seeking, tradition-keeping, or psychological manipulation. The same thing goes for business meetings. The "sense of the meeting" may obviously become a device of autocratic or bureaucratic control unless person and church fear the Lord and believe in the leadership of the Holy Spirit. Despite the abuses, the Quaker method of arriving at group decision without counting hands or voting is a significant legacy from Fox and early Friends. Other Christian groups have experimented with these methods. Even the use of mediation and consensus-building between labor and industry, or among nations of the world, reflects a partial appropriation of the *method.*

One must caution, however, that the mere establishment of rapport and communication, functional as this may be, is not the same as the correlation of individual and collective concern by the Holy Spirit. Thieves can be *en rapport.* Meditation and mediation are both methods that depend for their ultimate value upon the source of authority to which men and women subscribe. In the final analysis it depends upon whether the source of truth is human or divine. In an age heavily laden with sophistry, the call comes to get beyond *methods* of manipulation for social ends, to the reception of truth from God himself through the Living Word.

Notes

Introduction

1. Arthur O. Roberts, "The Concepts of Perfectionism in the History of the Quaker Movement" (B.D. thesis, Nazarene Theological Seminary, Kansas City, MO, 1951).

2. Arthur O. Roberts, "George Fox's Concept of the Church" (Ph.D. thesis, Boston University, Boston, MA, 1954), microfilmed by Graphic.

Chapter One

1. Rufus M. Jones, *George Fox: Seeker and Friend* (New York, NY: Harper, 1930), 6.

2. George Fox, *Journal of George Fox*, ed. John L. Nickalls, (Cambridge, UK: University Press, 1952), 1. This revised edition, with epilogue by Henry J. Cadbury and introduction by Geoffrey F. Nuttall, is used in most cases throughout the book, denoted simply as the "*Journal*." A few references are drawn from the Ellwood edition (henceforth referred to as "Ell. *Journal*"), which presents non-narrative material in more complete form than does the new edition. The Ellwood edition is cited from the *Journal* that forms volumes 1 and 2 of *The Collected Works of George Fox*, 8 vols. (Philadelphia, PA: Marcus T.C. Gould, 1831 reprint). In this series, volume 3 contains the polemics, *The Great Mystery* and *Saul's Errand to Damascus*; volumes 4, 5, and 6, *Gospel Truth Demonstrated*, which are popularly known as the "doctrinals"; and volumes 7 and 8, which contain the epistles. Reference is made to the works by volume and page, except for the epistles, which are noted by number to facilitate ready referral to any edition. Subsequent *Journal* references include the year for the same reason.

3. Ibid.

4. Ibid., preface by William Penn, xxxix.

5. Cited by A. Neave Brayshaw, *The Personality of George Fox* (London, UK: Hodder and Stoughton, 1884), 28.

6. *Journal*, 1-2; year 1635.

Chapter Two

1. *Journal*, 3; year 1643.

2. Ibid.

3. Ibid., 4; year 1644.

4. Ibid., 5; year 1646.

5. Ibid., 5-6; year 1646.

6. Ibid., 6; year 1646.

7. Ibid., 11; year 1647.

8. Ibid., 27; year 1648.

9. John Cyril Flower, *An Approach to the Psychology of Religion* (New York, NY: Harcourt, Brace & Co., 1927), 164.

10. Elbert Russell, *History of Quakerism* (New York, NY: Macmillan, 1943), 19.

11. For a study of the mysticism of Fox, see Rachel Knight, *The Founder of Quakerism: A Psychological Study of the Mysticism of George Fox* (New York, NY: George H. Doran, 1923). See also Rufus M. Jones, *Spiritual Reformers in the 16th and 17th Centuries* (London, UK: Macmillan, 1914). An illuminating little book by Lewis Benson, *Prophetic Quakerism* (Philadelphia, PA: Friends Book Store, 1944), emphasizes a contrasting, prophetic approach.

CHAPTER THREE

1. *Journal*, 19; year 1647.

2. Jones, *Seeker and Friend*, 4.

3. Cited by Russell, *Quakerism*, 12.

4. *Journal*, 19; year 1647.

5. Ibid., 22-25; year 1648.

6. Ibid., 26; year 1648. See Knight, *The Founder of Quakerism*, 111, for a psychological theory about Fox's blindness.

7. Ibid., 27; year 1648.

8. Ibid., 35; year 1648.

9. Ibid., 40; year 1649.

10. Ibid., 43-44; year 1649.

11. For an excellent study of the subject of healing in Fox's ministry see *George Fox's Book of Miracles*, edited with notes by Henry J. Cadbury (Cambridge, UK: University Press, 1948).

12. *Journal*, 49; year 1649.

13. Ibid., 51-52; year 1650.

14. Ibid., 65; year 1651.

15. Ibid., 70-72; year 1651.

16. Knight, *The Founder of Quakerism*, 110.

17. See Rufus M. Jones, "Psychology," in *New Appreciations of George Fox*, J. Rendel Harris, et al. (London, UK: Swarthmore Press, 1925). See also A. C. Bickley, *George Fox and the Early Quakers* (London, UK: Hodder and Stoughton, 1884), 55. Bickley considers Fox to have been "temporarily insane"!

18. *Journal*, 88; year 1651.

29. Ibid., 98-99; year 1652.

20. Jones, *Seeker and Friend*, 55.

21. Ell. *Journal*, vol. 1, 140. See the *Journal*, 103ff.; year 1652.

22. *Journal*, 112; year 1652.

23. A number of good accounts of early Quaker heroes exist, among them: Mary Agnes Best, *Rebel Saints* (New York, NY: Harcourt, Brace, and Company, 1925); Philadelphia Yearly Meeting, *Quaker Biographies* multiple vols. (Philadelphia, PA: Friends Book Store, 1910-1916); Frances Anne Budge, *Annals of the Early Friends* (London, UK: Samuel Harris & Company, 1887); and Jane Budge, *Glimpses of George Fox and His Friends* (London, UK: S. W. Partridge & Co., n.d.).

24. *Journal*, 130-131; year 1652.

25. Ell. *Journal*, vol. 1, 181; year 1653. See *Journal*, 161-164 for a variant version.

CHAPTER FOUR

1. *Journal*, 174; year 1654.

2. Ibid., 168; year 1653.

3. Ibid., 197-198; year 1655.

4. Jones, *Seeker and Friend*, 114.

5. *Journal*, 199-200; year 1656.

6. Ibid.

7. Ibid., 280; year 1656.

8. Ell. *Journal*, vol. 1, 300; year 1656.

9. Jones, *Seeker and Friend*, 101. I do not know if the inscription is still there.

10. Ell. *Journal*, vol. 1, 180-181; year 1653.

11. *Journal*, 252-253; year 1656.

12. Ibid., 264-265; year 1656.

13. Ibid., 254; year 1656.

14. Ibid., 481-482; year 1664.

15. Ibid., 491; year 1665.

16. Fred Eastman, *Men of Power* (New York, NY: Cokesbury, 1939), 147-148.

CHAPTER FIVE

1. See *Journal*, 101, 223, 268-269. See also Kenneth Boulding, *There is a Spirit: The Nayler Sonnets* (New York, NY: Fellowship Publications, 1945).

2. Jones, *Seeker and Friend*, 130.

3. *Journal*, 263; year 1656.

4. Ell. *Journal*, vol. 1, 298; year 1656.

5. See *Journal*, 422; year 1661. See also p. 519.

6. Ibid., 517ff.

7. In 1670, for example, William Penn was tried in a case in which the judge demanded of the jury a verdict of guilty; he locked them up without food or water until they should so act. When they resisted this threat, he fined them. In reviewing the case the Court of Common Pleas unanimously decided a jury could not be fined for its verdict. This decision became a bulwark of English liberty. See Russell, *Quakerism*, 95-96.

8. *Journal*, 554-555; year 1669.

9. Ibid.

10. Margaret Fell Fox's testimony in the preface of the Ellwood *Journal*, vol. 1, 57.

11. *Journal*, 611; year 1672.

12. Ibid., 592-593; year 1671.

13. Ibid., 609; year 1672.

14. Ell. *Journal*, vol. 2, 275.

CHAPTER SIX

1. Ell. *Journal*, vol. 2, 364-365; year 1691.

2. Ibid., 362-363; year 1691. The account is given by Thomas Ellwood.

3. Ibid.

4. See Cadbury's account in the *Journal*, 752-756.

5. Ellwood's account, Ell. *Journal*, vol. 2, 362-363; in the *Journal*, 759-760.

6. See Cadbury's account in the *Journal*, 752-756.

Chapter Seven

1. See Cadbury's epilogue for details regarding Fox's death and burial, *Journal*, 752-756. The excerpts from the legacy, unpolished in language and spelling, is cited from Vernon Noble, *The Man in Leather Breeches* (New York, NY: Philosophical Library, 1953), 286. It appears in fuller form in the Cambridge *Journal* (1911).

2. *Collected Works*, epistle 386.

3. *Journal*, 385; year 1660. See also *Collected Works*, vol. 6, 312-313.

4. *Collected Works*, epistle 14.

5. *Collected Works*, epistle 177.

6. John Jackson, *A Sober Word to a Serious People* (London, UK: 1651), 3. Cited by Rufus Jones, *Studies in Mystical Religion*, (London, UK: Macmillan, 1923), 461.

7. Saltmarsh, *Sparkles of Glory* (London, UK, 1648), cited by Jones, *Mystical Religion*, 455-56.

8. Cited by Budge, *George Fox and His Friends*, 102.

9. R. Newton Flew, *The Idea of Perfection in Christian Theology* (London, UK: Oxford University Press, 1934), 282.

10. *Collected Works*, vol. 4, 127.

11. Ibid., 128.

12. Ibid., 300-305.

13. *Collected Works*, vol. 5, 94.

14. Ibid., 140.

15. Cecil Eugene Hinshaw, "Perfectionism in Early Quakerism" (Ph.D. dissertation, The Iliff School of Theology, Denver, CO, 1943), 94.

16. *Collected Works*, vol. 5, 270-271; vol. 6, 439. Fox makes reference to Scriptures such as 1 Peter 1:15, 1 John 1:7, Daniel 9:24, and Hebrews 10:22 and 13:12.

17. Flew, *Idea of Perfection*, 291.

18. *Collected Works*, vol. 4, 128.

19. Ibid., 444-445.

20. *Collected Works*, epistle 260.

21. *Collected Works*, vol. 7, 237.

22. *Collected Works*, vol. 3, 487ff.

23. Isaac Penington, *Selections from the Works of Isaac Penington*, ed. John Barclay (London, UK: Darton and Harvey, 1837), prefix by Thomas Ellwood, xxv.

24. Ibid., xxviii.

25. Ibid., xxx.

26. Isaac Penington, *Works*, 4th ed. (Sherwoods, NY: David Heston, 1863), vol. 4, 210.

27. Ibid., 239.

28. Ibid., 257.

29. William Penn, *No Cross, No Crown* (London, UK: Edward Marsh, 1849), 33.

30. William Penn, *Journal*, vol. I of *A Select Series*, ed. John Barclay, 4th ed. (London, UK: Darton and Harvey, 1835), 265.

31. William Penn, *The Rise and Progress of the People Called Quakers* (Philadelphia, PA: Friends Book Store, 1855 reprint), 22-23.

32. Ibid., 82.

33. Robert Barclay, *An Apology for the True Christian Divinity* (Philadelphia, PA: Friends Book Store, 1908 ed.), prop. xi, sec. vii.

34. Barclay, *Apology*, prop. vii, sec. iii.

35. Ibid., prop. viii, 1.

36. See propositions iv and xii.

37. Cited by Budge, *Annals of the Early Friends*, vol. 1, 5.

38. Ell. *Journal*, vol. 1, 142; year 1652.

39. William Sewell, *History of the Quakers*, 5th ed. (London, UK: William Phillips, 1811), vol. 1, 91.

40. Cited by Budge, *Annals of the Early Friends*, no. 3, 4.

41. Ibid., no. 5, 5.

42. Ibid., 8

43. Ibid., no. 7, 4.

44. Ibid., no. 16, 4, 9. Cf. Romans 8:2 for biblical quotation.

45. Penn, *Rise and Progress*, 23.

46. See Boulding, *There is a Spirit*.

47. Sewell, *History*, 268.

48. Ell. *Journal*, vol. 1, 429; year 1661.

49. *Journal*, 357; year 1659.

50. Charles Evans, *Friends in the Seventeenth Century* (Philadelphia, PA: Friends Book Store, 1885), 626.

51. See the biography by W. R. Moody (New York, NY: Revell, 1900), 82; and Morgan, *The Ten Commandments* (New York, NY: Revell, 1901).

52. John Woolman, *Journal* (Philadelphia, PA: Friends Book Store, 1912 reprint), 253.

53. Joseph Bevan Braithwaite, ed., *Memoirs of Joseph John Gurney*, 4th ed. (Philadelphia, PA: Book Association of Friends, 1854), vol. 1, 102.

54. Joseph John Gurney, *Essays* (Philadelphia, PA: Henry Longstreth, 1856), 627-628.

55. *Discipline*, Yearly Meeting of Friends in Ireland (Dublin, Ireland: Webb and Chapman, 1847), xiii.

56. Geoffrey F. Nuttall, *To the Refreshing of the Children of Light* (Pendle Hill pamphlet no. 101, 1959). Accessible online at www.pendlehill.org/resources/files/pdf%20files/php101b.pdf. Nutall remarks in a commentary on Quaker ways, "Now that Friends have ceased to record ministers...." I presume his message is directed primarily to English Friends and to the nonpastoral Friends in Philadelphia. Friends groups that do not record ministers are in the minority.

57. *Faith and Practice*, Northwest Yearly Meeting of Friends (Newberg, OR: Barclay Press, 1987) 25-26. See also "Proceedings of the General Conference of Friends" held in Richmond, Indiana, 1887 (Nicolson, 1887).

58. Howard Brinton, in the *Register of Harvard University* (April 1951). See also his book *Friends for 300 Years* (New York, NY: Harper, 1952), in which he gives excellent analysis of the strands of thought that have interwoven the prophetic and mystical insights of Friends. He considered that the first half of the twentieth century was dominated by modernism, but he looked forward to a pattern of Quaker life in Quakerism's fourth century that will achieve a harmony of the mystical and prophetic. Brinton wrote from within the Conservative (nonpastoral) Quaker tradition.

59. Rufus M. Jones, *A Call to What Is Vital* (New York, NY: Harper, 1939), 108-111 and the whole of chapter 6.

60. Benson, *Prophetic Quakerism*, 508. Rufus M. Jones's interpretation of early Quakerism has been effectively challenged by a number of contemporary writers. Geoffrey Nuttall's studies of Puritanism have provided a renewed emphasis upon the English antecedents to the Quaker movement. In separate doctoral studies, T. Canby Jones and I (Arthur O. Roberts) have shown the basically evangelical Christology of Fox and have clearly differed from some of Rufus Jones's interpretations of the Quaker founder. Magazine articles evaluating Jones appeared along with other biographical material on the man. In one of the articles, appearing in *Friends Journal* (October 26, 1957), Wilmer Cooper suggests that Rufus Jones in his later years began to realize his views had

become too immanent, to the devaluating of God's transcendence and his offer of salvation.

61. Thomas R. Kelly, *A Testament of Devotion* (New York, NY: Harper, 1941), 65.

62. D. Elton Trueblood, *Signs of Hope in a Century of Despair* (New York, NY: Harper, 1950), 59.

63. Edward Mott, *Sixty Years of Gospel Ministry* (Portland, OR: private pub., 1947), 151.

64. "Report of the fourth Triennial Conference of Evangelical Friends," Denver, Colorado, 1956.

65. Arthur O. Roberts, *The Association of Evangelical Friends: A Story of Quaker Renewal in the Twentieth Century* (Newberg, OR: Barclay Press, 1975).

66. Winthrop Hudson, "Mystical Religion in the Puritan Commonwealth," *Journal of Religion* 28 (January-October 1948): 51.

67. Penn, *The Rise and Progress*, 20.

68. Ernst Troeltsch, *The Social Teaching of the Christian Churches*, vol. 2, Olive Wyon, trans. (London, UK: Allen & Unwin Ltd., 1950), 780.

69. *Journal*, 25; year 1648.

70. Ell. *Journal*, vol. 1, 237; year 1656.

71. *Collected Works*, vol. 4, 99-101.

72. Ibid., vol. 3, 596.

73. Ibid., vol. 4, 259-262.

74. *Collected Works*, epistle 91.

75. *Collected Works*, vol. 6, 478-479.

76. Richard Baxter, *The True Catholic and Catholic Church Described*, cited by Paul Elmer More, *Anglicanism* (London, UK: S.P.C.K., 1935), no. 4, 84.

77. *Journal*, 29-31; 1649. See also pp. 134-136, 331-332.

78. More, *Anglicanism*, no. 49, 91, citing Peter Cunning, a contemporary of Fox. See also Calvin's position as stated in the *Institutes*, book 1, chap. 7, sec. 4, cited by Barclay, *Apology*, prop. iii, sec. i, 73.

79. Cited by Barclay, *Apology*, 48-49.

80. Rachel Hadley King, *George Fox and the Light Within* (Philadelphia, PA: Friends Book Store, 1940), 165.

81. *Journal*, 194-195; year 1655.

82. Cited by Geoffrey Nuttall, *The Holy Spirit in Puritan Faith and Experience* (Oxford, UK: Basil Blackwell, 1946), 23.

83. Gerald Winstanley, *Works*, ed. George H. Sabine (New York, NY: Cornell University, 1941), 519. Citation is from "Law of Freedom."

84. See Benson, *Prophetic Quakerism*.

85. *Collected Works*, vol. 6, 228.

86. Ibid., vol. 5, 203, 264.

87. King, *Light Within*, 38; and Howard Brinton, *Friends for 300 Years* (New York, NY: Harper, 1952), 21.

88. *Journal*, 236-237; year 1658. Fox's paper is signed jointly by Edward Pyott and William Salt. See also Barclay, *Apology*, props. v and vi.

89. *Collected Works*, vol. 5, 266-267.

90. *Collected Works*, epistle 222. Italics mine.

91. *Journal*, 107; see also *Collected Works*, epistle 100.

92. *Journal*, 517; and preface, *Collected Works*, vol. 7, 14.

93. *Collected Works*, epistle 144.

94. Arnold Lloyd, *Quaker Social History, 1669-1738* (London, UK: Longmans, Green and Co., 1950). Chapter 9 provides a good treatment of the subject.

95. *Collected Works*, vol. 4, 123.

96. See Fox's paper, "A Distinction between the two Suppers of the Lord," *Collected Works*, vol. 6, 282-283.

97. Ibid.

98. Ibid

99. *Collected Works*, vol. 6, 209.

100. See Lloyd, *Quaker Social History*, 42-43.

101. *Collected Works*, epistle 64.

102. *Collected Works*, epistle 14.

103. *Collected Works*, vol. 6, 424; *Collected Works*, epistle 14.

104. *Collected Works*, epistle 29.

105. *Collected Works*, vol. 3, 381.

106. *Collected Works*, epistle 264.

107. Cited by William C. Braithwaite, *The Second Period of Quakerism* (London, UK: Macmillan, 1919), 360ff. See also Barclay, *Apology*, prop. x, sec. xxviii.

BIBLIOGRAPHY

In addition to books cited in the endnotes that support my text, I list below some that have been published since 1959, when *Through Flaming Sword* was originally released. My own writings relevant to the topic are noted separately, under "Selected Writings."

Barbour, Hugh, and J. William Frost. *The Quakers*. Richmond, IN: Friends United Press, 1988.

Barclay, Robert. *Barclay's Apology in Modern English*. Edited by Dean Freiday. Newberg, OR: Barclay Press, 1991. This is a more reader-friendly version of the older edition cited.

Early Prophetic Openings of George Fox. Philadelphia, PA: Tract Association of Friends, 1980.

Faith and Practice, Northwest Yearly Meeting of Friends, http://www.nwfriends.org/wp-content/uploads/2007/04/faith-and-practice-2003.pdf.

Foulds, Elfrida Vipont. *George Fox and the Valiant Sixty*. Philadelphia, PA: Friends General Conference, 1975, 1997.

Fox, George. *The Works of George Fox*. Edited by T. H. S. Wallace. Camp Hill, PA: New Foundation Fellowship, 1991. This is a new edition of the eight-volume set, comprising most of Fox's writing, first published in 1831. The editors include a helpful bibliography of books and journal articles.

Fryer, Jonathan. *George Fox and the Children of the Light*. London, UK: Kyle Cathie, 1991.

George Fox's Legacy. Edited by Charles and Caroline Cherry. Haverford, PA: Friends Historical Association, 2006. These papers from various contributors emanated from a 2002 conference celebrating the 350th anniversary of the Quaker awakening.

Gwyn, Douglas. *Apocalypse of the Word*. Richmond, IN: Friends United Press, 1986.

Ingle, H. Larry. *First Among Friends: George Fox and the Creation of Quakerism*. New York, NY: Oxford University Press, 1994. An extensive bibliography of primary and secondary sources includes a listing of Fox's writings.

Jones, T. Canby. *The Power of the Lord is Over All: The Pastoral Letters of George Fox*. Richmond, IN: Friends United Press, 1989.

Kolp, Alan. *Fresh Winds of the Spirit*. Richmond, IN: Friends United Press, 2007.

Punshon, John. *Portrait in Grey*. London, UK: Britain Yearly Meeting, 2006.

Sharman, Cecil W. *George Fox and the Quakers*. Richmond, IN: Friends United Press, 1991.

Spencer, Carole Dale. *Holiness: The Soul of Quakerism*. Milton Keynes, UK: Paternoster, 2007.

That Thy Candles May Always Be Burning: Nine Pastoral Sermons of George Fox. Camp Hill, PA: New Foundation Fellowship, 2001.

Williams, Walter R. *The Rich Heritage of Quakerism,* revised edition with an epilogue by Paul Anderson. Newberg, OR: Barclay Press, 2006.

SELECTED WRITINGS OF ARTHUR O. ROBERTS

Chapter in *American Quakers Today*, ed. Edwin B. Bronner (Friends World Committee for Consultation 1966, revised 1976).

Early Quaker Writings: 1650-1700, ed. with Hugh Barbour (Grand Rapids, MI: Eerdmans, 1973; Wallingford, PA: Pendle Hill, 2004).

Chapter in *Quaker Understanding of Christ and Authority*, ed. T. Canby Jones (Friends World Committee for Consultation 1974).

History of the Association of Evangelical Friends (Newberg, OR: Barclay Press, 1975).

Chapter in *Handbook of Church History*, ed. T. Downey (Oxford, UK: Lion, 1977; Grand Rapids, MI: Eerdmans, 1990; Minneapolis, MN: Fortress, 1995).

Tomorrow Is Growing Old: Stories of Eskimo Quakers (Newberg, OR: Barclay Press, 1978).

Chapter in *Quaker Views on Eschatology*, ed. Dean Freiday (Friends World Committee for Consultation, 1980).

Children of the Light, a musical, music by Dave Miller (private publication, 1983).

Chapter on Quakers in *Great Leaders of the Christian Church*, ed. John D. Woodbridge (Chicago, IL: Moody, 1988)

Drawn by the Light: Autobiographical Reflections (Newberg, OR: Barclay Press, 1993)

"The Vietnam Era, Evangelical Perspective," *Friends & the Vietnam War* (Wallingford, PA: Pendle Hill, 1998).

Robert Barclay's *A Catechism and Confession of Faith*, ed. with Dean Freiday (Newberg, OR: Barclay Press, 2001).

The People Called Quakers, booklet, 5th ed. (Newberg, OR: Barclay Press, 2006).

Messengers of God: The Sensuous Side of Spirituality (Barclay Press, 1996, 2006).

"Come in at the Door," in *George Fox's Legacy: Friends for 350 Years*, ed. Charles L. Cherry, Caroline L. Cherry, and J. William Frost (Haverford, PA: Friends Historical Association, 2006).

The Sacred Ordinary: Sermons and Addresses, esp. "Call to Holiness" (Newberg, OR: Barclay Press, 2006).

GEORGE FOX'S LIFETIME

Birth: July 1624

▼ 1630 ▼

1635 Fox's early childhood Christian experience

▼ 1640 ▼

1643 George Fox left community and family to wander about in a spiritual quest, sometimes debating religious issues with clergy.

1644 A literary contemporary, John Milton described England's situation as much bickering over religious matters.

1646 Fox trudged about the marshy fenland distributing money to needy widows and young married couples.

1647 Fox began to evangelize after being released from a season of temptations by the Light of Christ. Fox found reassurance that the tempter could be overcome "in and by Christ."

1648 With his spiritual trials behind him, Fox entered Nottinghamshire and began to preach among Ranters, Baptists, Independents, and other restless sectarians.

Fox supported himself as a shoemaker.

1649 Commonwealth executed King Charles I.

Fox was imprisoned for the first time.

▼ 1650 ▼

1650 Fox took over a church meeting where his doctrine of holiness challenged Calvinist doctrine.

Fox was imprisoned for the second time.

1651 In the Patrington area, Fox was beaten with a brass-bound Bible, and went without food for several days because people wouldn't sell him any food.

1652 Following his vision atop Pendle Hill, Fox's preaching "gathered to the Lord" crowds of Seekers and the influential Fell family of Swarthmoor.

1653 Fox was imprisoned for the third time.

Fox advocated a plan for marriage by which the couple should lay the matter "before the faithful," secure the clearance of church and relatives, and take one another in an appointed meeting.

1654 "Valiant Sixty" evangelists had covered the north country.

1655 The beginning of a new epoch in the ministry of Fox; approximately fifty thousand Quaker converts to Christ were organized into groups.

1655-1666	Fox spent much of his time in tangles with the law and in prison (his fourth imprisonment was in 1656).
1656	According to the Quakers' own records, as a result of these policies directed against Quakers "there were seldom fewer than one thousand in prison in this nation for truth's testimony."
Fox was released from Launceston Castle.
1656-1660	Fox held large meetings to rally people together and to lay the foundation for the organization of the church.

▼ 1660 ▼

| 1660 | Fox was arrested at Swarthmoor on charges of insurrection, and he was imprisoned for the fifth time.
Quakers had established themselves in nearly every colony in the new world.
The Commonwealth ended, the monarchy was restored. |
|---|---|
| 1662 | Fox was imprisoned for the sixth time, for refusing to take the Oath of Supremacy and Allegiance.
A specific act was passed against the Quakers, and Fox was rearrested at Swarthmoor Hall. |
| 1664 | Fox was imprisoned for the seventh time; his imprisonment began at Lancaster and was completed at Scarborough in September 1666. |
| 1665 | Great Plague in London |
| 1666 | The Great Fire in London |
| 1669 | George Fox married Margaret Fell, of Swarthmoor. |

▼ 1670 ▼

Dec. 1671	Fox was in Jamaica and began an almost twenty-year tour of the Quaker outposts
1673	Fox's mother died.
1673-1675	Fox was detained in Worcester prison in 1673—his eighth and final imprisonment. This was followed by a series of "skirmishes" with the law.
1677	Fox made ministry trips to Holland and Germany.

▼ 1680 ▼

1684	Fox visited Holland again.

Death: January 13, 1691, at 9:30 a.m.

His hardest labor finished, Fox preached at Gracechurch Street, London, on January 11, 1691, and two days later Fox left this life, in peace.